WEST GA REG LIB SYS
Neva Lomason
Memorial Library
DISCARD

# ATTRACTING BIRDS TO SOUTHERN GARDENS

Thomas Pope
Neil Odenwald
Charles Fryling, Jr.

*Foreword by*
Nancy L. Newfield

"Some Common Myths about Southern Birds" by
J. V. Remsen

*Paintings by*
John P. O'Neill
H. Douglas Pratt
Murrell Butler

Taylor Publishing Company
Dallas, Texas

*Designed by* Deborah Jackson-Jones

*Cover: Bluejay and painted bunting. House and garden, Mr. and Mrs. Caballero, garden design by Cynthia Cash.*

Copyright © 1993 by Thomas Pope, Neil Odenwald, and Charles Fryling, Jr.

All rights reserved.

No part of this book may be reproduced in any form without written permission from the publisher.

Published by Taylor Publishing Company
1550 West Mockingbird Lane
Dallas, Texas 75235

Library of Congress Cataloging-in-Publication Data

Odenwald, Neil G.
Attracting birds to southern gardens / Neil Odenwald, Thomas Pope & Charles Fryling, Jr.
p. cm.
Includes bibliographical references and index.
ISBN 0-87833-830-6
1. Gardening to attract birds—Southern States. I. Pope, T. E. (Thomas Everett), 1930– . II. Fryling, Charles. III. Title.
QL676.56.S68036 1993
639.9'78—dc20 93-7572
CIP

*Printed in the United States of America*

10 9 8 7 6 5

# Acknowledgments

The authors would like to acknowledge a large group of contributors to this book. During our early discussions, continuing deliberations, and the writing of this book, the authors enjoyed the support of many people who were willing to share freely their knowledge and expertise about bird and plant association. Many shared their most prized photographs and garden settings. Without this support we never could have covered such a large area of the country and included such widely diverse information in a single volume in the brief period of book preparation.

Leading the list of consultants who provided a wealth of information on birds, their habitats, distribution and behavior was Dr. James V. Remsen, Jr., ornithologist and curator of the LSU Natural Science Museum, which contains one of the largest bird collections in the world. In addition he contributed a chapter, "Some Common Myths about Southern Birds," was a principal reader, and on numerous occasions opened his naturalistic garden for our study and photography.

We are deeply indebted to three nationally acclaimed artists whose six bird paintings are first published in this book. These artists are Murrell Butler, Dr. John P. O'Neill, and Dr. Douglas Pratt. Their works have appeared in art galleries and highly prestigious bird guides and other publications.

The authors express their most sincere appreciation to Nancy L. Newfield for her foreword to this book. Nancy is recognized as a leading hummingbird authority in the United States, and is one of the few people permitted to band hummingbirds. Nancy has experimented with plants attractive to hummingbirds and has shared her knowledge and experience with bird lovers and gardeners throughout the nation.

Included in the book are photographs by some of the South's finest amateur bird photographers. Special acknowledgments go to C. Bernard Berry; Dr. Jacob Faust; Steve Hope; W. J. Turnbull; Max Parker; Charles Mills; Larry Raymond, who made available slides from the collection of the late W. B. Lonnecker of Shreveport; and Dr. James V. Remsen, who contributed bird photographs. Equally important to the success of this book were the individuals who contributed plant and garden slides. These include Hugh and Mary Palmer Dargan, Dr. William Fountain, Roger Kelley of Kelley's Photography, Dr. Earl Puls, Greg Grant, Felder Rushing, Dr. Benny J. Simpson, and Steve A. Frowine and Michael Dodge of White Flower Farms.

Special thanks go to those whose gardens are featured in this book. They include the ELsong Garden at the Emy-Lou Biedenharn Foundation, The Crosby Arboretum, Rex and Miriam Davey, Dan Gill, Richard and Jessie Johnson at the Caroline Dormon Nature Preserve, Doris Hope, Jeanne Lee, Lee R. McMillan, Middleton Gardens, Mississippi State University Campus, Robert Murry, New Orleans Nature and Science Center, Dr. Judith Patrick, Jim and Winkie Rector, Wm. Boatner Reily, San Antonio's Breckenridge Park, garden of the late Dr. Shewen Slaughter, Linda Schultz, C. C. Stewart, H. P.

Stewart Sr., and Jan Truitt at the Botanical Gardens of the University of North Carolina at Charlotte.

The authors acknowledge the untiring efforts of the editorial staff at Taylor Publishing Company. We are particularly indebted to Holly McGuire, our editor, for her patience and creativity.

LSU landscape architecture graduate students Douglas Baker and Hap Kern are acknowledged for their work on preparing the final drawings of the landscape plans used in the book.

Connie Graham and Diane Butler guided us in the preparation of the manuscript on the computer.

We sincerely appreciate the encouragement, support, and perseverance of our families, especially Doris Falkenheiner and Lucy Staring Pope.

Others who gave freely of their time and knowledge which aided in the preparation of this book are the following:

Sadik Artunc
Bonnie and Jules Bailey
Pat Butler
Mr. and Mrs. Rick Caballero
Sherline Z. Carver
Cynthia Cash
Van L. Cox
Dr. Catherine Cummins
Mary Palmer and Hugh Dargan
Marion Drummond
Carolyn and Jimmy Evans
Ann Faust
Dr. James F. Fowler
Dan Gill
Bob Green
Jeff Green
Dr. L. M. Hardy
John Harris
Mr. and Mrs. Ray Havard
Jane Honeycutt
Marion Jackson
Margie Jenkins
Loice Kendrick
Helen Leslie
John D. Mayronne
Charlene Nelson
Nancy L. Newfield
Dr. E. N. O'Rourke
Geri Patrick
Dr. Alton Pertuit
Carolyn Phillips
Lou Riddle
Bruce Sharky
Marilyn and Bob Shaw
Doris Shell
Dorothy Shell
Sara and Dennis Shell
Ruth Glynn Sims
Oscar Slade
Larry Smart
Dr. Gail M. Smith
Marcelle and Albert Staring
Marianna Tanner
Dr. Bob Thomas
Judith Toups
Martha Waldron
Shirley and Don Walsh
Joan Wharton
Wayne Womack

# *Table of Contents*

# Foreword

Extravagant gardens and an appreciation of wildlife are honored traditions in the South. And, though Southern ecosystems are bountiful, the allure of greater rewards inextricably intertwines the lives of a myriad of wild creatures with an ever increasing assortment of cultured lands.

Southerners hold traditions long after the reasons for their emergence have become obsolete. But the value of landscaping for the benefit of wildlife has become more worthwhile today than it was during the eras of the great naturalists of the eighteenth and nineteenth centuries. John James Audubon commented on the drastic alterations that had been made to the vast Southern forests by the late 1820s.

The pace of our sophisticated modern life brings the tranquility of the natural world into sharper focus. We seek solitude and solace in the simple lives of creatures that remain as simple as their progenitors. We seek peace among wildlings that are innocent of human imperfections of guile and malice.

The custom of feeding birds has grown to support an industry, but feeding wild birds and other wild beings can only carry one part of the way back to a more elemental lifestyle. Many of us have found that we enjoy far greater satisfaction by creating habitats that sustain a multiplicity of wild creatures without forcing them to accept our proffered provisions. And, many of us have found that we achieve as much pleasure from creating as we do from observing. We have also found that using Nature's own foods to attract wildlife is infinitely more gratifying than simply scattering our store-bought seeds.

And who better to guide us than the authors, three men who have devoted their professional and private lives to the enhancement of all habitats natural and otherwise?

Thomas E. Pope, retired Horticulturist from Louisiana State University, spent his early childhood in Washington Parish, Louisiana, an area rich in the diversity of plants and wildlife. As a youngster, he wandered through the woodlands where he became aware of the huge assortment of native plants and birds—he knew where the various species of birds nested and the habits of wild turkey, quail, and many songbirds. These early experiences greatly influenced his career choice of ornamental horticulture. After he earned a Ph.D., his entire career, spanning over thirty-five years, has been devoted to teaching and research. Tom and his wife, Lucy, have developed a special interest in recent years in attracting and photographing birds at their Baton Rouge home.

Neil Odenwald, Professor of Landscape Architecture at Louisiana State University, grew up in the Mississippi delta, where large tracts of land had been cleared for single crop agriculture. Although Neil's primary interest during those formative years was in growing plants, he experienced the abundance of bird life. Thirty-five years of work in landscape architecture and horticulture have further heightened his sensitivity and interest in landscape design. As with Tom, attracting birds to his home grounds has added a new and special dimension to Neil's gardening pleasures in recent years.

Charles F. Fryling, Jr., Associate Professor of Landscape Architecture at Louisiana State University, spent his childhood in Texas and Pennsylvania. Although Charles's formal education was in landscape architecture, he has been an avid bird watcher all of his life. Charles has devoted much time and energy as a professional advocating strong conservation measures that protect and enhance all forms of wildlife in both natural and manmade landscapes. Over the past thirty years, Charles has received considerable acclaim for his nature photography, much of which includes birds in their natural habitats. Charles and his wife, Doris, travel extensively, viewing, studying, and photographing birds. Both have served in administrative capacities in the Audubon Society, the Sierra Club, and many other conservation organizations.

While the use of plantings to attract wildlife is not novel, the incorporation of design elements is refreshing. Too often, an advantageous shrub or perennial is planted where nothing else is growing rather than as a part of a pleasing landscape. With *Attracting Birds to Southern Gardens,* we have an aesthetic approach to wildlife diversity in our own comfortable surroundings.

NANCY L. NEWFIELD
METAIRIE, LOUISIANA

# Introduction

The South is blessed with an abundance of plant life, ranging from narrow and broadleaf evergreens to deciduous trees, shrubs, vines, and ground covers. The great diversity of climatic conditions, from the hot, arid regions of the western parts of Texas and Oklahoma to the cooler, higher altitudes of the Blue Ridge and Appalachian Mountains and, finally, to the warm, moist climate of the coastal plains of the Deep South, result in a wide variety of plant materials native to the area. More than 50 million Americans enjoy gardening in their leisure time, and gardening in the South has been popular since colonial times, as is evident by the many beautiful public and private gardens in the region.

Many of our native plants have been threatened with extinction by various practices such as single-crop agricultural methods, clear cutting of forests, urbanization, industrial and agricultural pollution, and a combination of these and other factors. Yet native plants offer so many advantages compared to exotic, imported species. Over the millennia, native plants have survived and thrived because of their tolerance of or resistance to the region's insects and diseases. In addition, they are acclimated to the temperature changes that occur during the year and are adapted to the regional soil and water conditions.

Introduced plants have many outstanding landscape features, but often require frequent sprays for pest control. Chemicals used to control these problems add to soil, air, and water pollution of the entire ecosystem. By proper selection

*Eastern Bluebird* (Sialia sialis) *by Murrell Butler*

and understanding of the growth requirements of native and exotic plants, it is possible to create a landscape that has interest throughout the year and that offers contrasts in size, shape, color, and texture. With careful selection and placement of plants, required maintenance in the landscape can be greatly reduced. There should be consideration not only of the beauty present when the plant is in flower, but also of the added enrichment of plant form, leaf and stem texture, fall color of leaves, and winter color of berries, tree trunks, and branches.

Birding is the second most popular leisure activity in the United States, enjoyed by more than 37 million people. When combining gardening and birding, you can have the best of both pastimes. Birds can be attracted to the home landscape by providing four basic needs: food, water, shelter, and a place to nest and raise young. Food and water can easily be supplied with well-stocked feeders and waterers. Just these two elements will attract birds. By the addition of plants which provide cover, nesting sites, and protection, many more birds and species of birds can be attracted to your yard.

In the South, millions of individual birds are permanent residents. These include the cardinal, mockingbird, blue jay, Carolina chickadee, tufted titmouse, Eastern bluebird, American robin, several woodpeckers, and many more. In addition, countless millions of birds, including rose-breasted grosbeak, scarlet tanager, many vireos, warblers, and flycatchers, migrate through the area to and from their winter homes in Central and South America. Many millions of birds also choose to spend their winters in the South, flying back to their breeding grounds in the upper South and more northern areas in spring.

Among the winter residents in the South are the American goldfinch, hermit thrush, pine siskin, purple finch, white-throated and other sparrows, cedar waxwing, and others. Summer residents of the South that spend their winters in Central and South America include the Baltimore and orchard orioles, painted and indigo buntings, purple martin, prothonotary warbler, red-eyed vireo, and the amazing ruby-throated hummingbird.

Regardless of the time of year when the birds are present, they can still be attracted to the garden when the basic life-sustaining needs of food, water, and shelter are provided. In developing your garden or landscape, you should consider the needs of the birds you hope to attract. For example, fruiting and seeding trees and shrubs are important during late fall, winter, and early spring. During this time insects, which are needed by many birds, are less numerous or absent, and fruit- and seed-eating birds need great supplies of food to keep warm and survive. Even in spring and summer, fruit and seed are still used as a source of food by many birds.

We hope in this book to direct gardeners and birders to the plants that can be used in garden and landscape plans that will provide bird habitats and that will conserve and encourage the cultivation of native plants. Well-planned landscapes can be both aesthetically pleasing and functional as well as serving as a refuge for declining wildlife and native plant populations.

*Wood Thrush* (Hylocichla mustelina) *by John P. O'Neill*

# Landscaping to Attract Birds

Attracting birds and other forms of wildlife to the home grounds is as old as our earliest desire to have personal spaces of solitude and close encounters with nature. Literature, art, and music through the ages have made frequent references to man's love of this form of wildlife and the very high position which birds have been given. All cultures have been attracted to the "birds of the field," the backyard songbirds, and even the more exotic birds caged in elaborate aviary spaces. Birds have been invited to our landscapes for the purpose of adding special meaning and enrichment in the form of animation, music and other special sounds, color, and that unique "life" to our outdoor spaces which can be supplied by no other landscape element. Those landscapes where birds find a safe and happy refuge are normally healthy bits of nature. Encounters with these landscapes satisfy these deep-seated longings which most of us have for being in and a part of the natural world. In a given region, there are few sites totally without permanent resident birds. However, through deliberate planning of both the new and renovated landscapes, the number of birds attracted to the garden can be greatly increased. Studies indicate that the population of birds in rural, natural landscapes of the country are much higher than the numbers found in urban settings. Consequently, conscious efforts must be exercised to incorporate into any

*In the ELsong Garden at the Emy-Lou Biedenharn Foundation, Monroe, Louisiana, one of the objectives was to attract birds to the garden. Quoting Miss Emy-Lou's memoirs, "This is a winged garden. . . Red-breasted robins run up and down the lawns for their morning worms. Tiny darts of vivid yellow pop out of the swaying pouch-like nest in my sycamore tree. Oriole songs pierce the quiet dawn. The blending of bells, of quiet lawns, and brick walls all blend together."* (Photo by Roger Kelley)

landscape designed to attract birds those fundamental elements they require: food, water, shelter, cover and space for living. The technical information for each of these elements is covered in other chapters of this book. The purpose of this chapter is to incorporate these elements in general design guidelines which will help us in planning gardens that will attract birds.

Attracting birds to a garden is relatively simple and inexpensive. There may be a few instances when a conscious effort is made to design nearly every detail to attract birds. In most cases it is much more appealing and practical to make the attraction of the birds just one of several objectives for your overall landscape development. Of course, food, water, cover and space for living must be a paramount concern if birds are to visit the garden in large numbers.

The very essence of gardening is planning a space for the introduction of plants and other elements which stir emotions and cause us to become more intimately involved in our outdoor spaces. The incorporation of diverse plant forms, colors, and textures are the same qualities which provide the "bones" of a habitat for birds and the seasonal foods which will eventually attract them to our garden settings. Seldom will a garden, even when it has been exclusively designed for birds, provide all of the essential needs of birds throughout the year. Consequently, even for those homeowners whose attitudes toward attracting birds are the major theme of their gardens, design will normally go much further in making a space more enticing by staging feeders of many types, waterers, perches, and other components to supplement the seasonal food supplied by plants in order to improve the overall appeal for birds.

The size and complexity of gardens designed for birds can vary from that of the smallest and most modest inner-city dwelling where a single feeder is placed in a tree or shrub outside a window, to the "average" sized suburban subdivision home which is one of many similar dwellings, to the huge country sites that include vast open lawns and woodland edges. All of these kinds of spaces can become attractive bird habitats and at the same time add to the overall quality of our environment. Urban plantings are supplementing the rural habitats, much of which are being cleared and converted to single-crop agricultural enterprises. The current emphasis on expanding urban forest, the "greening" of our cities through major tree planting programs, and educational programs directed toward reducing the use of harmful pesticides in our gardens are other measures being used to make our urban centers more attractive to birds. Our individual garden efforts become an important part of the basic fabric of this much larger and extremely complex ecosystem. So no site is too small or too large to be used as a habitat for birds. The basic concept of attracting birds can be incorporated into every design regardless of style, mood, income level, and within any regional context.

*Mockingbird eating fruit of blueberry.*

## *Design Factors*

**Bird Species.** Among the first decisions we have to make is to determine which species of birds we wish to attract to our gardens. The choices are the resident birds that stay all year, the winter birds, summer birds, and pass-through migrants. The permanent resident birds of an area are usually territorial. Examples include cardinals, mockingbirds, and blue jays. Others, such as the ruby-crowned kinglet, may come in winter as singles or in small groups, while still others, like the cedar waxwings, often travel in large flocks. The ground feeders, like some of the sparrows and thrushes, require open ground spaces but want dense cover close by. The purple martins require large open spaces for flight and will

*The interior space of this home is perfect for bird viewing. In the background, the woodland planting utilizes many native species. In the foreground, the magnolia offers excellent cover and perching places for the birds between visits to the feeding and watering stations near the house. Note that the glass in the windows is tilted downward to reflect ground instead of sky and plants. This helps reduce instances of birds crashing into the glass. Several small windows rather than one large plate of glass also reduces the number of collisions into glass.* (Davey, Baton Rouge)

*A combination of native plants in open spaces and woodland edges provide birds with shelter, nesting, and food in this Beaufort, South Carolina garden.*

*A dense background border of natives and mixed woody and herbaceous foreground plants define this Baton Rouge garden space. The vine-covered arbor in the background doubles as a bird-watching blind. Tropical flowering plants are introduced from the greenhouse to attract hummingbirds.* (Patrick, Baton Rouge)

be attracted to houses only in relatively large expanses of open space. So birds of choice become one factor to consider in determining the final layout of a garden which is designed for birds.

Observations indicate that regardless of availability of food, a bird's prime need is protection and cover in the form of shrubbery and other dense plant life. Without protection, birds will visit feeders only in desperation, dart back to their protected perches, and will not become a viable part of the close-range landscape.

**Edges.** Try to create as many edge plantings as possible in your landscape. In most gardens, only the perimeters of a site are used, as the rectangular shape of the property is repeated with filler plants. Incorporating long curving beds helps to maximize the linear footage in a relatively small space. The addition of island plantings within the larger spaces is another way to incorporate more edging to an otherwise square lot. The island plantings help conceal portions of the grounds and add interest to the landscape. The edges can be further improved by making several layers within the plant borders to create edges within edges. Both horizontal and vertical layering help to increase edge volumes in a development. In the South, where conditions are optimum for fast plant growth, there is often a tendency to pack too many plants within a given space. Plants growing on the edges of beds are much more apt to flower and produce a greater abundance of fruit than those placed in thick layers within wide borders.

**Layering.** Use plants of varying heights to provide a layering effect for diversity in the vertical dimension. Tall trees provide canopy above. Intermediate-sized trees and large shrubs form the middle layers while the ground layer is completed with small, low-growing shrubs and ground-cover plants. In the lower South, plants grow rapidly and, if allowed to grow freely, will end up completely filling a space and forming only dense thickets. Here birds have little space to maneuver. Although some dense growth is desirable for a higher degree of protection, most plants do not produce flowers and fruit in this type of heavy, competitive, crowded condition. Both in well-established woodland settings and in new designs, a conscious effort should be made to select and group plants which provide distinct layering. In the older plantings, shade-tolerant understory trees and shrubs can be added to an already established tree canopy. For new developments, you must start out with sun-loving plants and gradually introduce the more shade-tolerant plants as the upper story cover develops.

**Open Spaces.** To add interest in the landscape, volumes of spaces should vary in size and shape, or configuration of the outside edges. Such terms as opening and closing spaces, concealment and revealment, convey the idea that the spatial sequence can be greatly varied and spaces become roomlike in character to enhance the quality of the outdoor spaces. Too often spaces are merely large, open, monotonous volumes lacking interest within themselves. Meandering spaces, can increase the amount of edges in a given landscape and provide places where the more sociable and friendly birds can be near the home, while in the farther removed areas the more skittish species can be accommodated. Some spaces can be relatively free with little or no plant massing, while in other areas plants can be combined to form dense bosques of plant growth.

**Plant Diversity.** The region is blessed with an abundance of plants which attract birds. With careful planning and selection there can be plants producing food attractive to some birds for virtually the entire year. Once the general garden layout has been defined by paths and edges, there is a huge pallet of species available within the context of good design principles to fulfill the needs of any garden scheme. If the skeleton of design is created by clearly defined boundaries of fencing, paths, surfacing and other architectural elements, the final planting design can normally accommodate a great diversity of plant species attractive to birds. If a garden lacks a strong sense of structure formed by hardscape materials, it often comes across as a collection of horticulture specimens with little design integrity.

Personal preferences also influence plant choices for a garden design. For example, one individual might prefer hollies, which would attract

*In dry areas of the region, such as parts of Texas and Oklahoma, plants similar to those used in the Sunken Garden in Breckenridge Park in San Antonio make an interesting garden. Plants used in this garden for Xeriscape (water-conserving) design include salvia, firebush, crybaby tree, lantana, hibiscus, yuccas, trumpet vine, and cacti.* (Photo by Greg Grant)

*Centers devoted to preservation, research, and wise use of native species are at many locations in the South. At the Crosby Arboretum near Picayune, Mississippi, "living" laboratories contain more than 700 plant species in such diverse landscapes as pitcher plant bogs, beech-magnolia forests, evergreen hammocks, cypress and gum swamps, pine savannas and hills, flatwoods, and bottom-land woodlands representing the native flora of the Pearl River drainage basin in Mississippi and Louisiana.*

a broad spectrum of bird species. Another might find that, although there are all sorts of varieties, using hollies alone as the dominant species would not have enough year-round appeal. Fortunately, the diversity of plants attractive to birds in the region is so great that there should be no problem finding plants to satisfy personal needs, those which birds enjoy, and selections which fit the design scheme.

**Seasonal Variation.** Strive to have enough diversity among the plants to provide striking seasonal changes in the garden. Incorporate both evergreens and deciduous woody plants to provide strong seasonal contrasts. A concentration of one plant type, either deciduous or evergreen, might result in strong features at only one period of the year, whereas a balanced mixture of both deciduous and evergreens will provide continuing change among the plants. Even when specialty gardens are designed to attract particular birds, like the hummingbirds, there should be sufficient "permanent" plants to give the garden a sense of structure and the qualities needed for seasonal change. A single type, such as a predominance of perennials, can result in a rather drab winter scene. Many gardens are at their best during spring and early summer when there is an abundance of flowering plants. However, choosing plants that are attractive to birds can extend this period of appeal through the entire year. Deciduous plants that exhibit striking autumn foliage color and bare winter branching are often overlooked.

**Proximity.** Viewing birds at close range from within a building can be an exciting experience. Too often gardens are designed in such a way that birds feel insecure near the house. They dash up to the building in desperation to collect food placed in feeders and then are off to their more protected habitats in far away places out of view. If a number of the appropriate plantings are placed near the house, some birds will perch near a window and reveal other full-color and "personality" traits. What is more beautiful than a cardinal sitting on a twig of a river birch tree or on the branch of a dogwood right outside a breakfast room window in the dead of winter? By selective pruning, the forms of trees and shrubs can be modified to slightly interrupt views to the more remote parts of the landscape instead of screening background plant life. This touch can make the view more appealing than a completely open view of the same space. Provide small patches of lawn near the house to accommodate the ground feeders. Thrashers, which

*This woodland edge (summer) is not more than twelve to fifteen feet from the indoor living area. Birds seem to be in touching distance. Growing in Caroline Dormon's beloved Briarwood Nature Preserve are wax myrtle, tree huckleberry, Carolina buckthorn, yaupon, and strawberry euonymus.*

*The same edge at Briarwood in winter. At this time of year, bird feeders and feeding station in the center of the woodland edge are apparent. Richard and Jessie Johnson, Nature Preserve curators, have recorded twenty-six species of birds at these stations during a typical winter.*

exhibit their stately, elegant profiles as they gather insects in a lawn, are especially fascinating. Animation provided by birds like the purple martins, which need open flight pathways, can be appreciated at a great distance. However, having birds near the indoor spaces where the details of their particular habits and characteristics can be revealed, adds wonderful qualities to a well-designed garden.

## Garden Styles

When thinking about a garden design, one of the first matters to consider is the character or mood that appeals to you. We often refer to this as garden style. The final mood will be definitely affected by personal needs, desires, and economic ability to install and manage your area. The style can range from the one extreme of being nearly totally untamed nature to the other extreme of highly sophisticated elegance such as found in a French or Italian Renaissance formal garden, to anywhere in between—or combinations of both. Fortunately, birds are not influenced by garden styles as we perceive them, and there are those birds which can be attracted to any man-made landscape. Regardless of style, birds will visit gardens which include food, water, protection, and space for living.

For the purpose of this book, five different and rather clearly defined styles or specialty gardens will be explored. Seldom would there be an occasion when any one of the styles would be used in its purest form. Traditional garden styles are the ones generally accepted by landscape architects and other garden designers who work with clients to help with the general parameters for garden design. Each style is normally modified to fit a particular homeowner's needs and the requirements of the yard. Once the style or mood is clearly defined, then the design process can be completed, with a master plan evolving which best reflects the desires and needs of a given client.

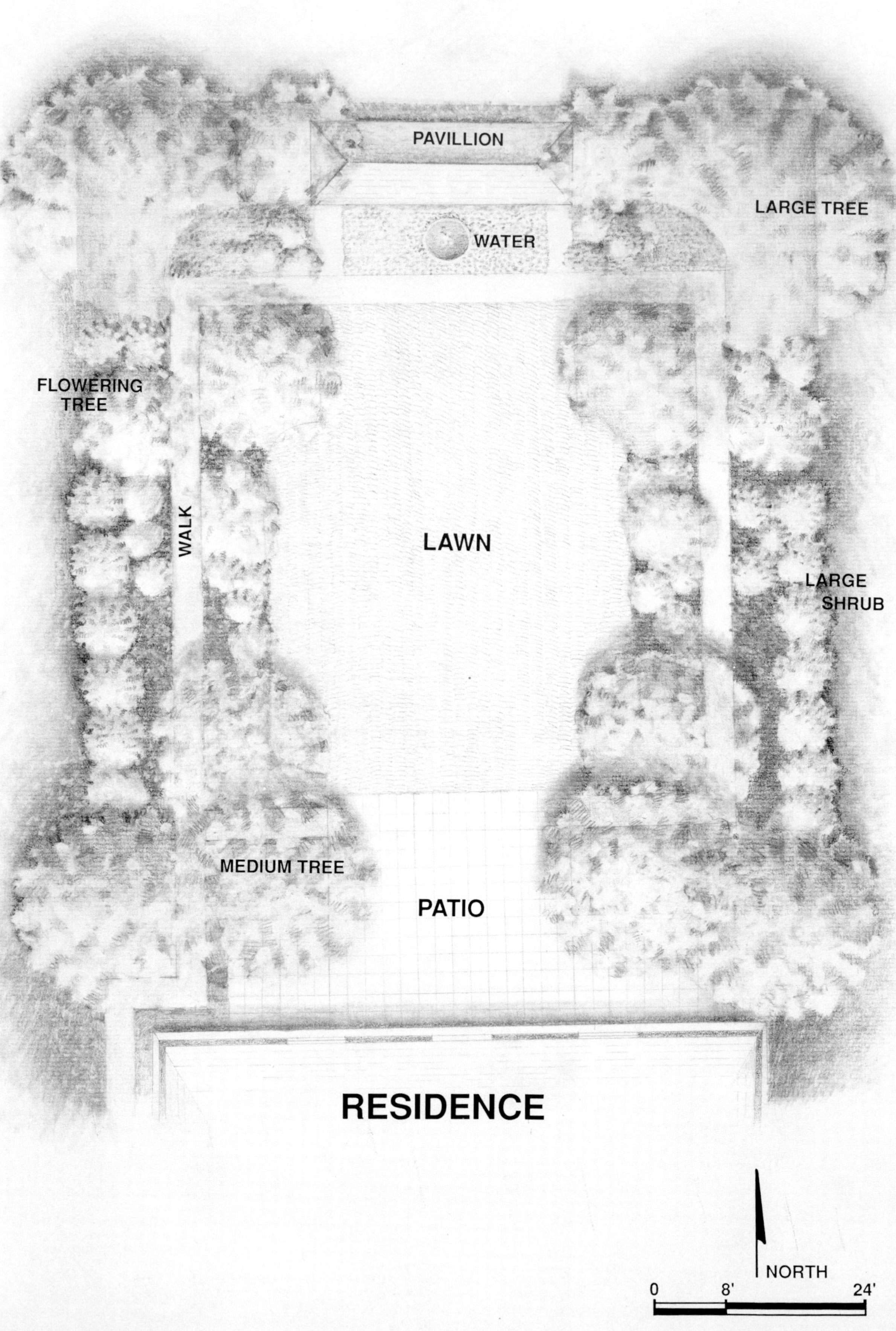
PAVILLION
WATER
LARGE TREE
FLOWERING TREE
WALK
LAWN
LARGE SHRUB
MEDIUM TREE
PATIO
RESIDENCE
NORTH
0
8'
24'

## *Formal Gardens*

Dating back to the earliest civilizations in Persia and Egypt, gardens were inspired from wall paintings, carpets, and tapestries. Many contemporary gardens are still being greatly influenced by the geometric arrangement of elements from early gardens. Great emphasis is placed on surface pattern, where rich paving is normally used to provide structure for this widely held classical style. While a formal garden might be within the context of a larger, less formal layout, formal gardens normally have strong, defined boundaries within which the walks, planting beds, and plants themselves provide a highly ordered pattern with a strong emphasis on symmetrical balance among the garden elements. Traditionally, such terms and elements as parterre, maze, Tudor knot garden, clipped and shaped topiary plant forms, and strong axial design characterize the elegance demonstrated in most formal designs. The earliest parterre garden was designed for the queen of France by Mollet in the sixteenth century. This highly disciplined, patterned style has been used through the centuries to show man's ability to tame and control nature, provide strict order in nature, and link the building architecture to the surrounding landscape.

You might think that a classical garden would impose excessive regimentation and limit the range of habitats attractive to birds. This need not be the case, for within such design there is usually ample room for personal expression and freedom to use a relatively broad spectrum of plants. The formal garden does not have to be a static, monotonous space. However, strong structured pattern does indeed lend itself to a clearly defined design intent. Once the layout has been well defined architecturally by such materials as brick, concrete, or stone paths and other paving, raised planting beds, statuary, furniture, pools,

*Formal: Formal design is characterized by a strong central axis with the repetition of the same plant materials on either side of the axis. Paving helps to designate a strong pattern. (See lists at end of chapter for plant selection.)*

*This small enclave in a formal garden utilizes a great diversity of plants, with a bird bath as the focal point of the design. Hummingbird plants include pentas, impatiens, hibiscus, cleome, and salvia.* (McMillian, New Orleans)

*In this New Orleans garden, the plant materials complement the garden structures. The clipped, upright 'Savannah' hollies and the informal planting of background cherry laurel offer food and shelter in this formal setting. The boxwood parterre encloses another fruiting holly, the dwarf 'Burford.'* (Reily, New Orleans)

*Formal, axial garden design layout provides an opportunity to introduce a wide diversity of plants in this Charleston, South Carolina garden.*

fountains, and other water features, then plants attractive to birds can further reinforce the strong pattern. The design can be completed with carefully selected evergreens and deciduous plants which are also attractive to birds. These plants can also be expected to provide seasonal color and other special interest throughout the year.

An alternative within this style is to structure the formality with architectural elements (walls, paths, planting beds, water and other forms of garden embellishment) which define the mood intended, and then introduce a much freer, more relaxed planting scheme within this formal framework. With this scheme the gardener can incorporate a wide assortment of fruiting and flowering plants, even to the point of making it a horticultural or botanical collection. Plants can also be allowed to grow naturally without the heavy-handed pruning normally associated with formal gardens.

Safe, traditional plants which seem quite appropriate for these more disciplined designs include cherry laurel, ligustrum, photinia, wax myrtle, red cedar, and many of the evergreen hollies. These plants, all attractive to birds, either as clipped hedges or natural forms, can provide the boundaries, screening and background for other plants. Intermediate-sized plants attractive to birds that might be included in a formal garden include abelia, barberry, dwarf burford holly, cotoneaster, nandina, old roses, and the mahonias. When it comes to low, clipped border plants, the traditional favorites—boxwood, dwarf yaupon, euonymus, dwarf azaleas, and sometimes flowering perennials and the herb edge plants—are primary choices. These may provide edges and some cover, but little food for birds.

*Formal/Informal: A transition between the formal and informal design, this scheme is typical of many suburban home sites. It utilizes plant massing around the perimeter of the property and features a large expanse of open lawn to accommodate a purple martin house.*

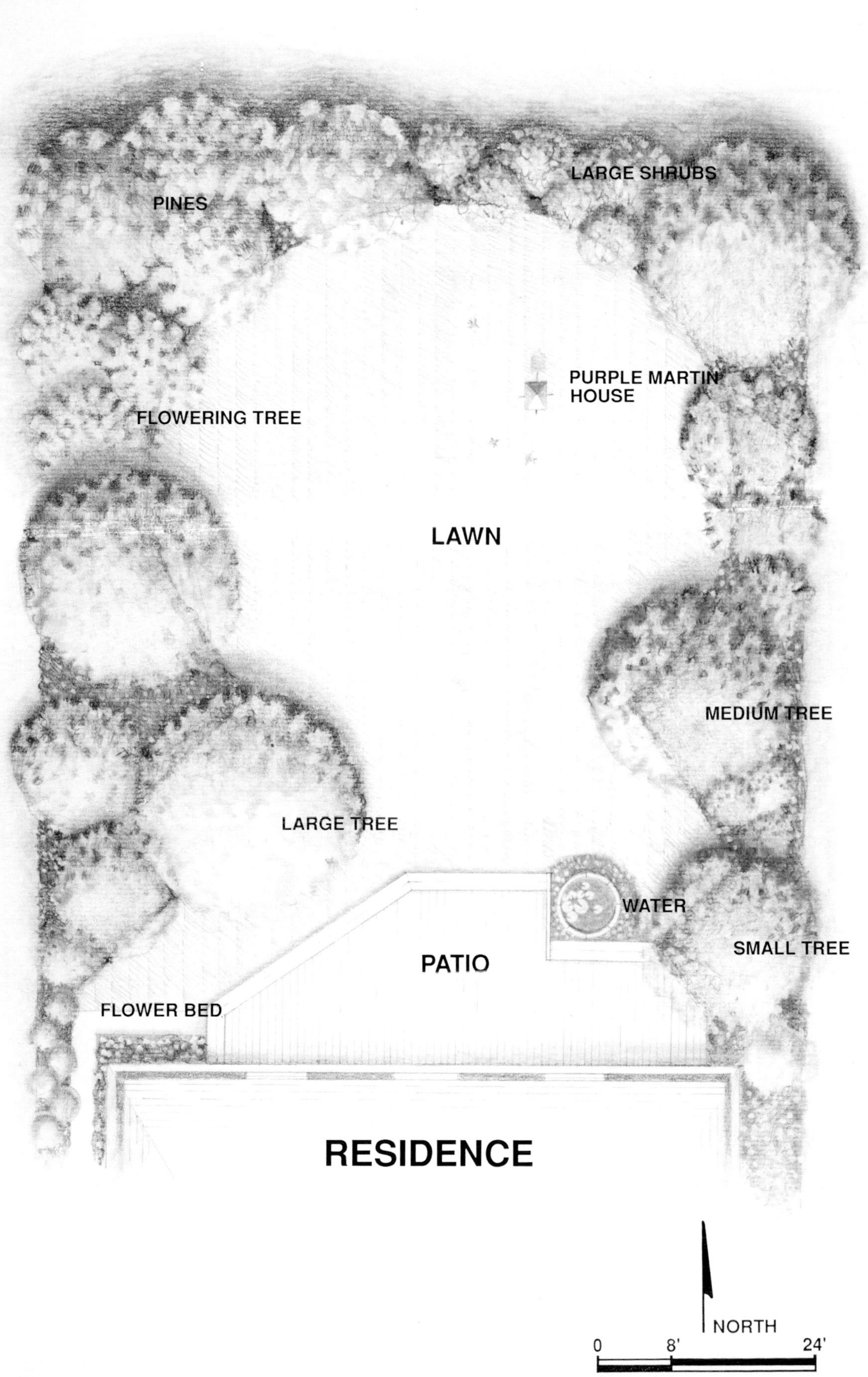
LARGE SHRUBS
PINES
PURPLE MARTIN HOUSE
FLOWERING TREE
LAWN
MEDIUM TREE
LARGE TREE
WATER
PATIO
SMALL TREE
FLOWER BED
RESIDENCE
NORTH
0
8'
24'

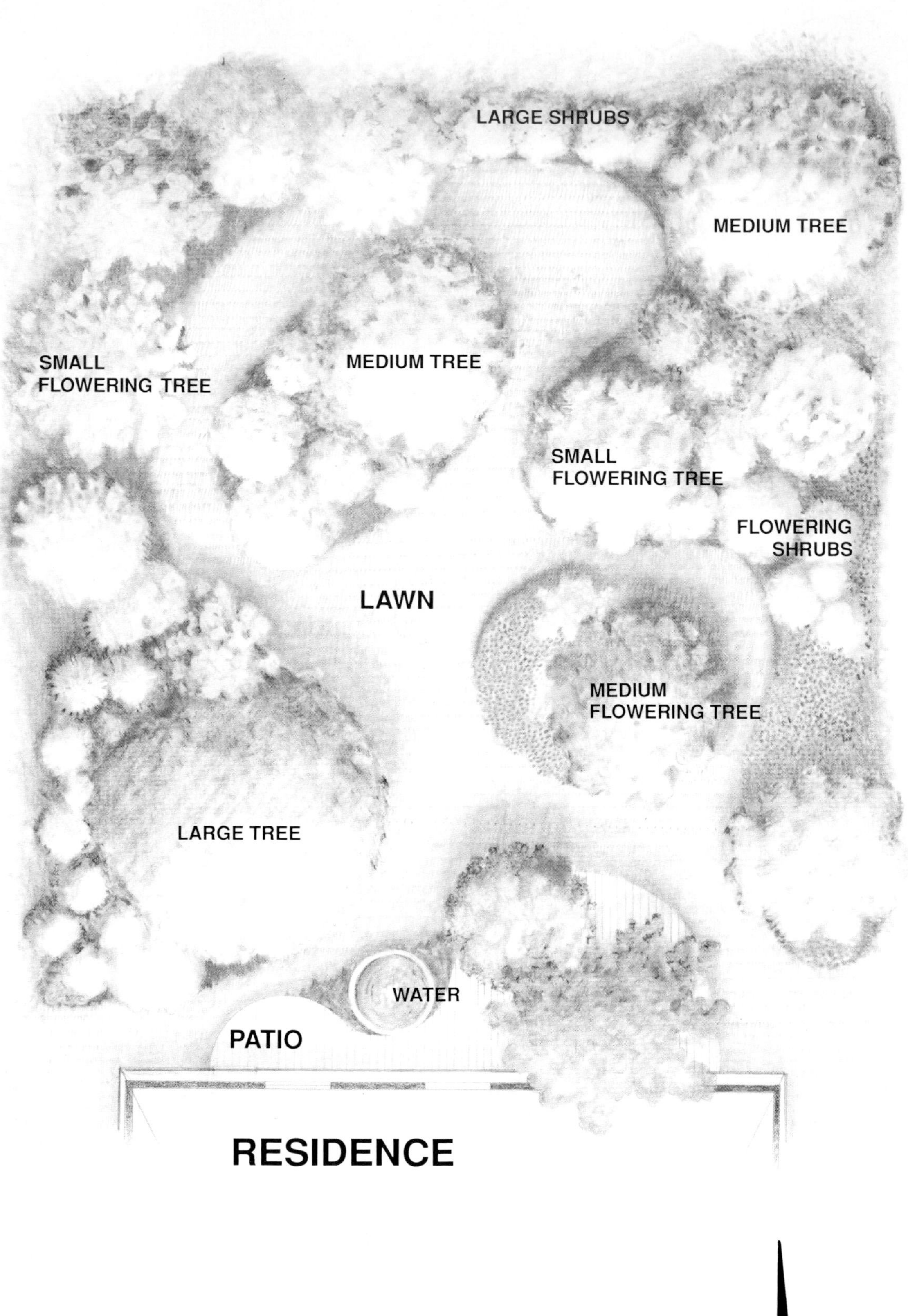
LARGE SHRUBS
MEDIUM TREE
SMALL
FLOWERING TREE
MEDIUM TREE
SMALL
FLOWERING TREE
FLOWERING
SHRUBS
LAWN
MEDIUM
FLOWERING TREE
LARGE TREE
WATER
PATIO
RESIDENCE
NORTH
0
8'
24'

## *Informal Gardens*

This garden style denotes a more casual arrangement of materials and is derived from a close observation of nature and the natural processes. Still relying on man's dominance in the manipulation of both plants and nonliving materials, there is more blending of the architectural framework with plants than we associate with the formal gardens. Plants are allowed to perform as they would in a more natural setting. No less designed than a formal garden, and requiring as much or more skill and sensitivity for design than a "formal" garden requires, this type garden provides a mood of pleasing interface with nature. For over a century English designers have been masters at this type of design. Such noted designers as William Robinson and Gertrude Jekyll of the last century and contemporary designers John Brooks, Penelope Hobhouse, and Rosemary Verey have designed numerous gardens which provide a wealth of inspiration about how gardens can be merged with nature and yet provide a strong sense of personal identity.

This style provides for a pleasing blending of the native, introduced, and even exotic species. Diversity of plant species and freedom to grow naturally, within limits, characterize this design. In addition to plants, other natural materials, including aggregate-surfaced paths, stone, wood, and water, are widely used to provide a more harmonious blending with nature.

Not to be mistaken as a style which requires no maintenance, these gardens do indeed require considerable attention. With such accelerated growth of plants in the South, especially in the coastal areas where the growing seasons are long and there is an abundance of rainfall, pruning is required relatively frequently. Maintenance need not be as tightly scheduled as with a formal garden, and days or even weeks do not make a lot of

*Informal/Freeform: This informal design with curvilinear lines provides maximum edging for the introduction of many species attractive to birds. Concealment created by the two island plantings adds interest and variety.*

*Bridging the formal and informal, the curvilinear edges of this Memphis garden incorporate a layering of plants, from the formal, clipped hollies to the freer, more natural forms of mixed evergreen berrying plants.*

*The flow of garden spaces in this Baton Rouge garden is enhanced by the center restriction of plants to form garden "rooms," which are given further definition and enrichment by a background of both native and introduced plants.* (Lee, Baton Rouge)

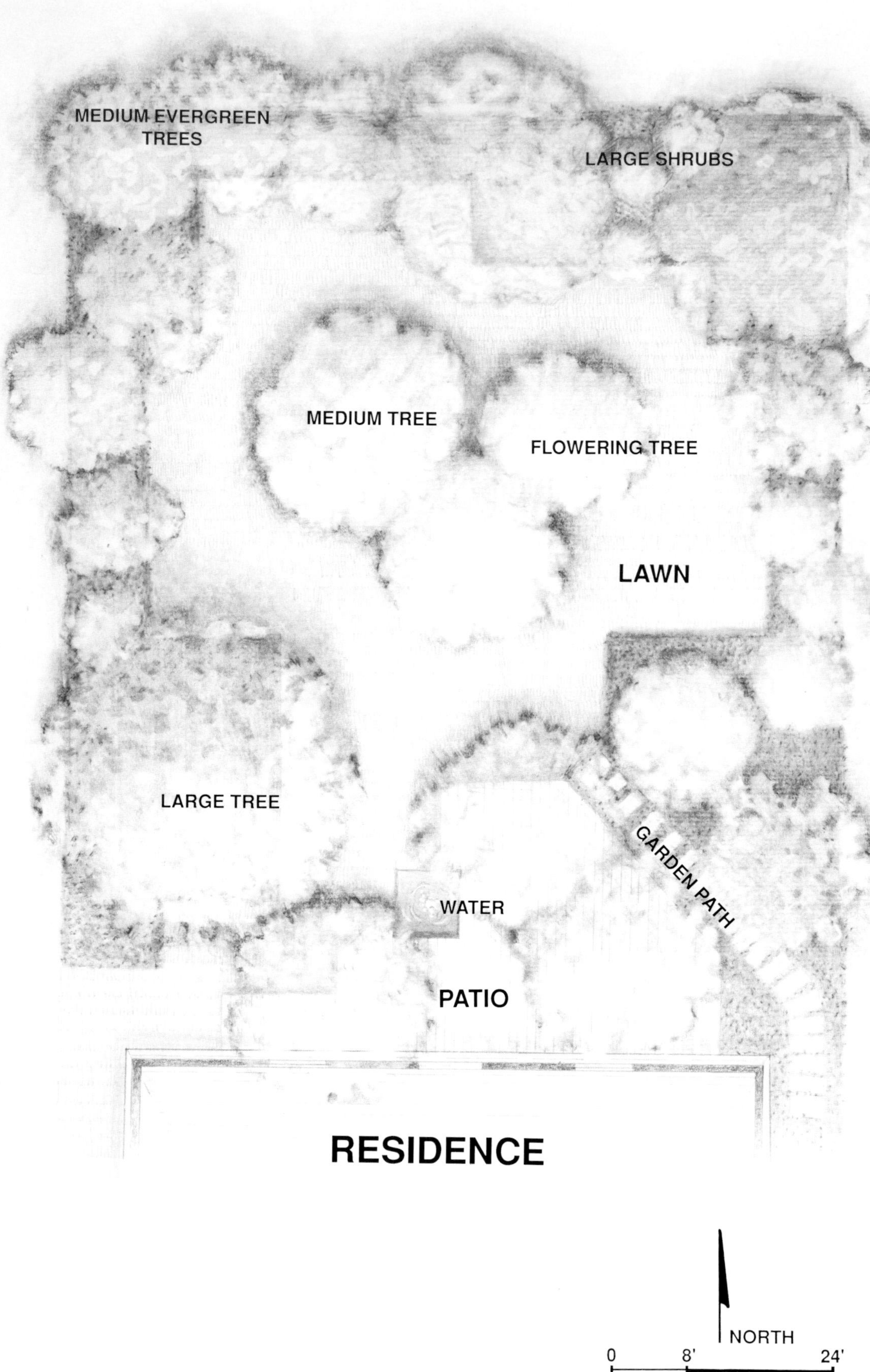
MEDIUM EVERGREEN TREES
LARGE SHRUBS
MEDIUM TREE
FLOWERING TREE
LAWN
LARGE TREE
GARDEN PATH
WATER
PATIO
RESIDENCE
NORTH
0
8'
24'

*On these large naturalistic grounds, the bog was retained to accommodate native Louisiana iris and other wetland plants. A mowed path is maintained adjacent to the woodland edge, which contains native trees and shrubs that are attractive to insects and wildlife.* (Slaughter, Baton Rouge)

difference in the final timing of many horticultural tasks. Plant sizes and competition among plants must be kept in check to insure that the various species produce flowers and fruits as expected. Only if this style is clearly understood and managed properly will there be noticeable labor saving over the reputed high-maintenance requirements of the formal gardens.

In informal gardens, individual specimens of many different species can be incorporated to provide year-round habitat and food for birds. Single-species plants repeated in drifts help to provide unity within the garden. As with all designs, plants are chosen within the concepts of correct scale and proportion to the garden space.

*In this model, the space is defined by straight lines. The island planting and the great length of border plantings allow for the introduction of a large assortment of bird-attracting plants as well as add interest to this rear garden.*

In the region, some of the traditionally popular "bird" plants might indeed fill a space if growth is allowed to go unchecked. Endless lists of plants with contrasting and pleasing colors, forms, and textures are available for this garden style.

## *Naturalistic Gardens*

Closely associated with the informal style noted above, this style denotes an even closer tie with the indigenous landscape. Each part of the region has its own regional expression and association of plants and other natural features such as unique climatic conditions, water, rock, and topography. These elements can be creatively used to shape and further enhance the overall character of the garden. From this context you can create a garden that clearly emphasizes the overall spirit of the area. It might be the semitropical gardens along the coast, the drier gardens of Texas and extreme coastal edges, or the more temperate landscape ecosystems of the upper South. From these larger "landscapes" are carved out intimate garden spaces which often further characterize the unique qualities of the region. Preserving the existing native flora and other features of a region is surely a worthy goal in the design of any garden. This type of gardening follows the current trend of emphasizing environmental stewardship.

For this garden style we normally rely heavily on native plants already on a site. Sometimes, a new, totally natural landscape scheme is planned; more often a particular site is chosen because of its inherent natural features—plants, interesting topography, rock and other natural phenomena. Many times, gardens are carved out from the site by selectively deleting underbrush and other undesirable plants. To these settings are added plants and other elements according to personal preferences. Some portions are often kept dense to provide cover for birds, while other areas might be clear-cut to form full-sun meadows. This introduces still another kind of natural landscape experience.

*The bird viewing station in Mountain Lake Sanctuary and Gardens at Lake Wales, Florida, overlooking a naturalistic pond surrounded by native flora.*

*The Louisiana Nature and Science Center in New Orleans is an excellent naturalistic demonstration garden. Many elements at this center could be duplicated in the home grounds in a small urban setting. A driftwood water feature, bird feeder, and an abundance of flowers to attract hummingbirds are featured. This photograph was taken from the indoor viewing room.*

For this scheme, a good knowledge of plants and their expected performance as well as sound artistic judgment are essential to ensuring that plants are both ecologically and aesthetically appropriate for the setting. Associated with this style is a lot of experimentation, even for the most skilled designer and plantsman. The harmonious blending of the native flora characterizes these garden settings. Naturalistic gardens provide opportunities for a unique layering and hierarchy in the use of plants. The tall-growing trees form the canopy, smaller trees form the intermediate layer of foliage canopy, and the low-growing, more sprawling shrubs and ground covers provide a low layer which helps to reduce undesirable plant growth. Plants used in drifts can add interest to the spatial quality of a naturalistic site by providing divisions that function very much like rooms of a house. Anticipation and discovery of what lies beyond can add a special sense of mystery and romance to a woodland garden. With careful grouping plants that direct viewing through the trunks of trees and down vistas, small spaces will appear to be much larger and secrets can be revealed in an orderly, planned sequence. Both evergreens and deciduous plants should be incorporated into this garden to insure strong seasonal contrasts in colors, textures, and forms.

Surprises, the appearance and disappearance, and reappearance of many herbaceous (non-woody) plants, add a lot of spontaneity to gardens. While the element of surprise is a natural phenomenon associated with all gardens, it is a special feature of the naturalistic garden style. Some of the plants have fleeting flowering periods, while others, like spring bulbs, flower for several weeks but have persistent foliage for another two months or longer. Because there is usually a buildup of soil-enriching humus, reseeding and self-generating from underground stems commonly occur. Reseeding insures that plants will find their best "home" sites and perpetuate themselves. Birds greatly accelerate the self-generating process by spreading seeds. Some plantings need to be intensified to give a stronger emphasis, while in other places heavy competitive growth may need to be eliminated to make room for the more desirable woodland species to fully develop. Self-seeding and allowing plants to grow where they can flourish is one way to reduce the maintenance requirements of a garden.

You can provide a strong unifying element to a natural woodland look by making paths surfaced with gravel, pine straw, bark, or other natural occurring materials. Such passageways encourage deeper exploration into the interior of the woodlands where the more timid birds might be found. In addition, benches, water, rocks and stone groupings, and other nonliving garden elements can help to provide the appropriate scale for human enjoyment in what might otherwise be a relatively large, poorly defined forest. Small, detailed plantings which further enrich the woodland experience are often added along paths and other close-in viewing areas.

For bird lovers, this garden style offers many opportunities and challenges. Normally, for the planting-design phase of the design work, the natives alone can provide a range of rich plants—from the tall, space-enclosing trees and shrubs down to the most intimate and detailed ground covers—which can satisfy nearly every need for attracting birds. The natives of a region have proven their worth over time and really belong to the area because of their tolerances to plant pests and extremes in climatic conditions. However, there are many introduced species which perform much like the natives. A plant's character of growth and ability to perform well within a naturalistic setting should make many plants serious candidates for the naturalistic garden. Regardless of how random and natural plantings will appear, the designer should have a particular character or image in mind. The final picture should closely resemble the overall character of the area, as if the landscape were not manipulated by the designer. Although nature might appear to be in control, man's presence is required to maintain a balance among the natural elements.

Such gardens cannot go unattended for long periods, especially in the lower South, where plant growth is so rampant. Frequent pruning and even the relocation of certain plants are normal maintenance requirements. This attention may not be at the same frequency and at the same intensity as required with the more formal gardens. The natural processes should be clearly observed and controls placed at given periods to insure that there is a reasonable balance among the plantings which provide food and shelter for birds.

*The woodlands of this rural subdivision were cleared just enough to accommodate the house, drive, and small hummingbird plantings around the home of a distinguished ornithologist.* (Remsen, St. Gabriel, Louisiana)

## Wild Woodland Gardens

As the name implies, this garden style truly celebrates nature, with all its ecologically associated elements, as the garden theme. "Gardens" normally denotes an ordered arrangement of natural materials, but in this style natural habitats are often staked out as they were by the earliest settlers and designated as a garden, where native species provide most of the components of the site. Henry David Thoreau, John Muir, Rachel Carson, and others have inspired us by their writings and conservation sensitivity to have a deeper appreciation for our untamed woodlands.

Pieces of the bigger natural areas can be created or claimed as our garden retreat. Natural evolution of the habitat is normally allowed to go at its own pace. Actually, considerable changes occur over a period of time as sites evolve through natural succession. Little or no attempt is made to arrange or rearrange plants according to any preconceived artistic or natural design guidelines. You merely take what nature has to offer and enjoy the benefits of the natural setting. Even modest additions or deletions affects the sites. Most people find that living within a wild garden in the purest sense does not fulfill their cravings for hands-on gardening. Consequently, plants, especially the herbaceous, flowering species, which perform well in the rich woodland soils in shaded places, are often added to further embellish the natural growth of the area and furnish the more ephemeral qualities so essential to our gardens.

*At the entrance of this home set in a woodland landscape, informal plantings are used to attract hummingbirds and to add accent and color.* (Remsen, St. Gabriel)

*In wild gardens, most of the existing plants are retained, eliminating only enough vegetation to allow for the introduction of a greater diversity of species and opening the site for paths and sunlight necessary for the growing of specially selected plants and small patches of turf and flowering plants.*

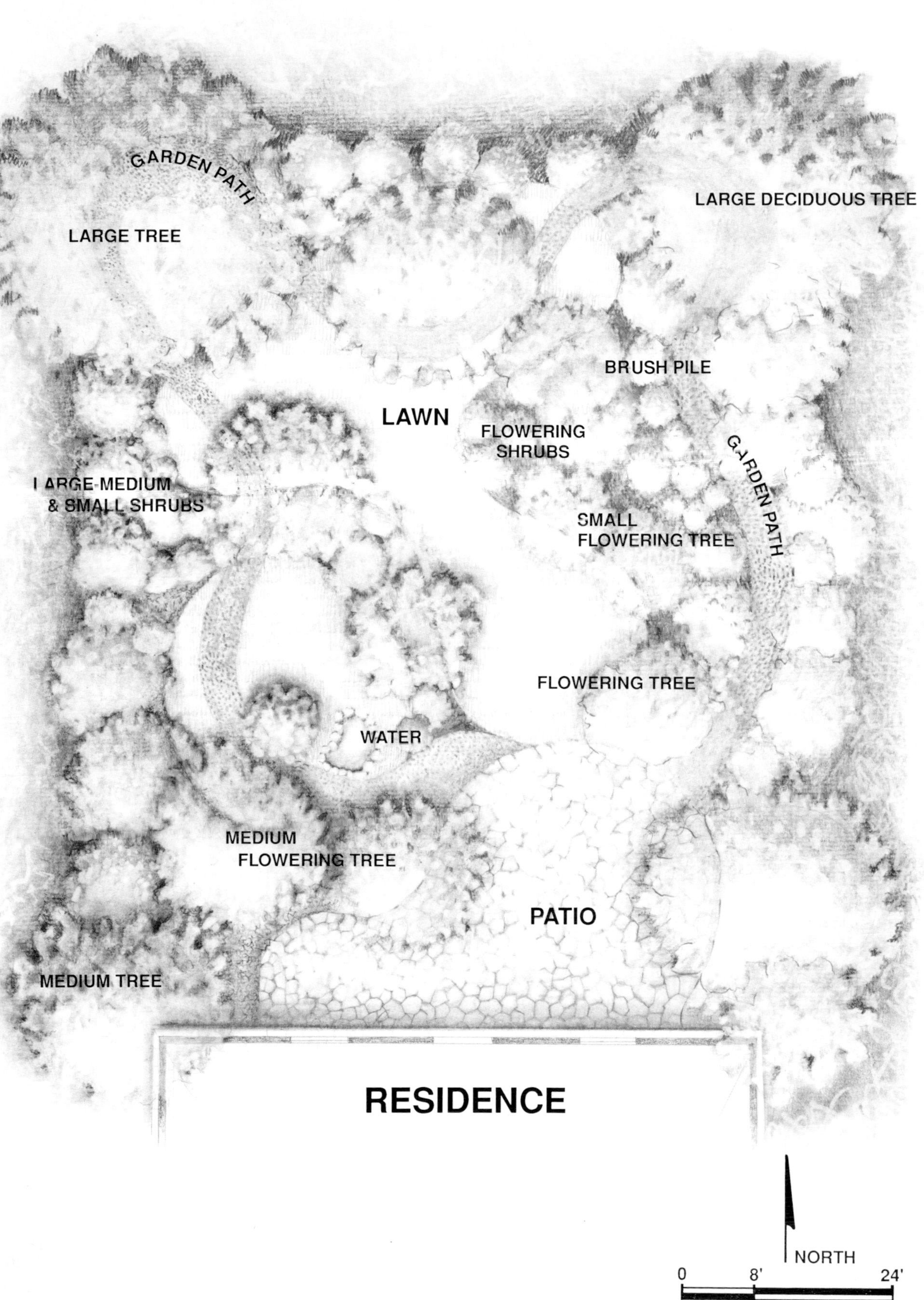
GARDEN PATH
LARGE TREE
LARGE DECIDUOUS TREE
BRUSH PILE
LAWN
FLOWERING
SHRUBS
GARDEN PATH
LARGE-MEDIUM
& SMALL SHRUBS
SMALL
FLOWERING TREE
FLOWERING TREE
WATER
MEDIUM
FLOWERING TREE
PATIO
MEDIUM TREE
RESIDENCE
NORTH
0
8'
24'

The characters of wild gardens vary greatly from region to region, depending primarily on the climatic conditions of the area. For the coastal area with its abundance of moisture and long growing season, the wild, untamed naturalistic garden goes through a period of junglelike growth that is nearly impossible to penetrate, but it is a wonderful habitat for birds. Even here, food might be somewhat scarce, except on the edges. Patience is required for the early years, until an upper canopy is formed to help crowd or shade out a portion of the understory growth. In the more arid parts of the region, growth takes place much slower because of the drier conditions and often less-fertile soils. However, even under such conditions, plants produce an abundance of flowers, fruit, and berries for birds. Between the two extremes are the woodland and forest lands of the more temperate region of the upper South. Given a choice, most of us would probably select a part of the region in the upper South for this type of garden. There seems to be a better balance in soil fertility, moisture, and more controlled plant growth, which makes living in a natural setting more comfortable and rewarding.

The tough, free-spirited native plants are the backbone for this garden experience. Each region has its unique flora which provide food for both the resident birds and the migratory spe-

*In early spring this upland wild landscape features coral honeysuckle, native Louisiana iris, buttercup, lyre-leaf salvia, and other wild flowers. The Japanese honeysuckle on the old fence row provides nectar for hummingbirds and fruit in fall for many birds. There are several layers of plants in the background.* (Murry, Simpson, Louisiana)

*At Middleton Gardens in Charleston, South Carolina, this wild swamp garden is referred to as the "lost link" in the sequence between formal and informal garden design.*

cies, which feed for shorter, specific periods on the available food supply. The natural weathering processes which take place in a woodland become an important part of these wild, naturalistic sites. All parts of dead plants should be allowed to decay and form the hunting ground for birds which feed on insects in the decaying wood. The humus aids in the regeneration of a self-sustaining landscape.

Paths surfaced with natural materials like bark, gravel, and pine straw are used to provide controlled access in order to preserve the forested area. The native plant life and introduced plants, water, rock outcroppings, topography, and diversity of the spatial experience are just a few of the elements which might be featured in a wild, woodland garden.

One goal in working with naturalistic sites is to create a self-sustaining landscape. Today there is a lot of emphasis being placed on those landscapes which are self-sustaining and require only a minimal amount of maintenance in the traditional sense of managing a viable garden. With water becoming so scarce in parts of the region and pesticides being carefully scrutinized, especially by bird lovers and at many natural preserves, self-sustaining landscapes may offer the safest haven as bird habitats. Strong water conservation measures as practiced in Xeriscape design tend to encourage a dominance of the native plant species. Birds play a major role by distributing seeds of these plants over a site. When seeds fall in places where germination, growth, and development can take place, then new species may be added. In unfriendly territory, seeds do not germinate, or if they do, plants do not develop to maturity and gradually fade out.

## Specialty Gardens

Gardeners sometimes desire to attract a particular bird or group of birds to their yards. While the gardens noted above will be successful in bringing a wide diversity of birds, especially the passerine (song) birds, there are other specialty gardens worthy of consideration. There are the **open meadow gardens,** filled with wildflowers and grasses and open vistas that attract many birds in search of insects feeding on the grasses and other sun-loving plants. Birds of the open fields like the bluebird, meadowlark, American goldfinch, and Eastern kingbird are examples of those attracted to the large open sites. Open meadows are maintained by mowing and controlled burning at specific times of the year as a means of interrupting the natural succession

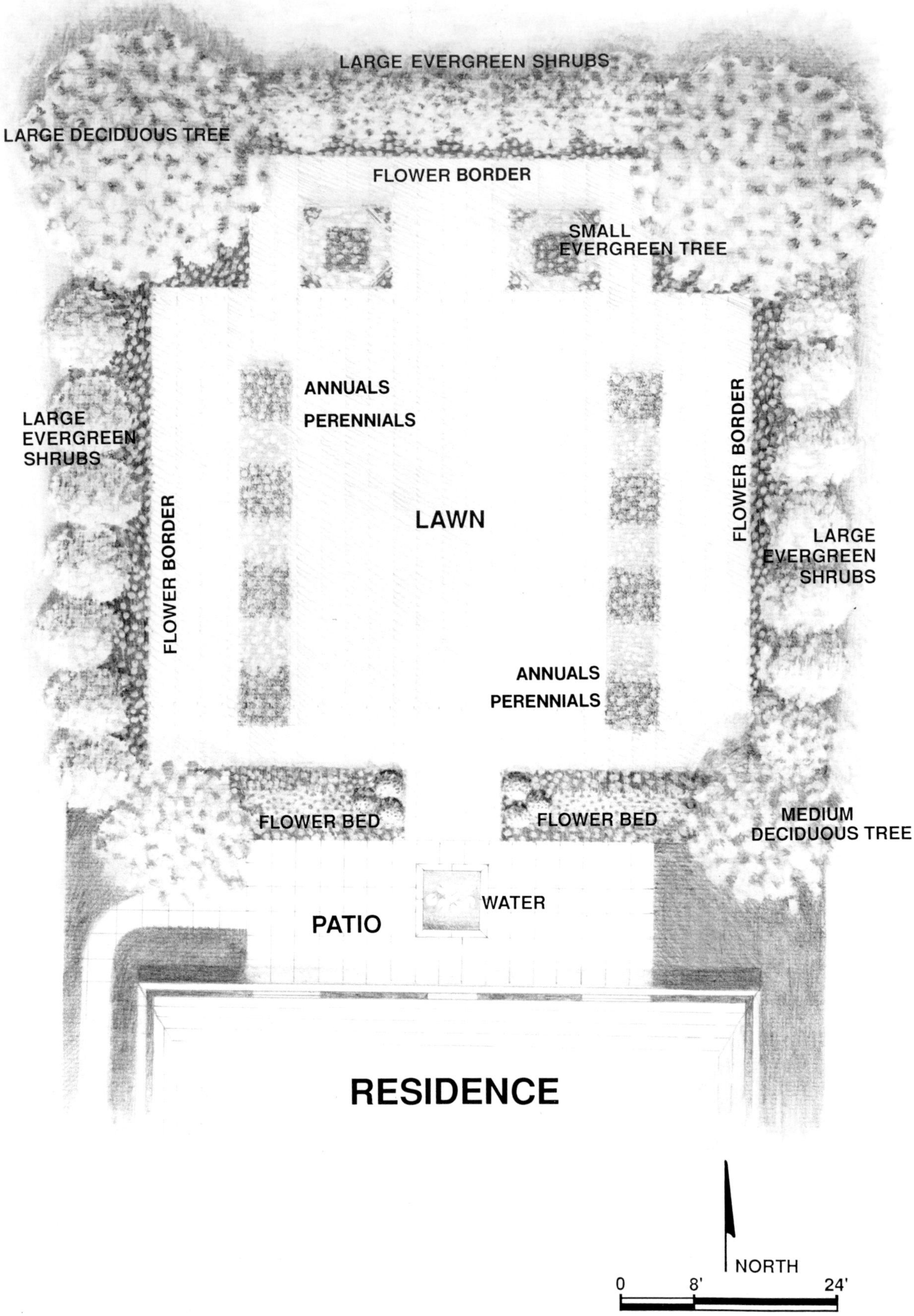

LARGE EVERGREEN SHRUBS
LARGE DECIDUOUS TREE
FLOWER BORDER
SMALL EVERGREEN TREE
ANNUALS
PERENNIALS
LARGE EVERGREEN SHRUBS
FLOWER BORDER
LAWN
FLOWER BORDER
LARGE EVERGREEN SHRUBS
ANNUALS
PERENNIALS
FLOWER BED
FLOWER BED
MEDIUM DECIDUOUS TREE
WATER
PATIO
RESIDENCE
NORTH
0 8' 24'

*Formal/Specialty: In a formal garden layout where there is an abundance of sunlight, many hummingbird plants can be incorporated into a design where there are clearly defined edges and planting beds. Border hedge plants provide food and habitat for other species of birds.*

through which natural landscapes evolve. Wading birds like the egret, heron crane and others associated with marshy sites and the wet edges of large ponds provide interest at considerable distances in rural settings. These gardens normally require large sites and are beyond the scope of this book, but are worthy of concentrated study and experimentation. Work on large sites will normally require the expertise of a biologist and special plantsmen because of the complexity of maintaining a balanced, attractive habitat.

A relatively inexpensive specialty garden which is also easy to incorporate into a larger garden setting is a **hummingbird garden.** Such a garden is filled with a broad range of flowering annuals and perennials, but may also contain flowering trees and shrubs. Typically, these gardens, often referred to as cottage gardens, include flowers that have a high nectar content from midspring through fall. Hummingbirds might be present in large numbers only for a portion of the peak flowering season, normally from March into October. However, several species of western hummingbirds migrate to the coastal areas of Texas, Louisiana, and Mississippi during the winter and need flowering plants for food.

The design of hummingbird gardens can vary greatly, from small patches of herbaceous flower-

*An herbaceous border of seed-producing plants, including seed-producing grasses and sunflower.*
(Mississippi State University campus.)

*A small urban garden designed to feature an abundance of flowering plants that attract hummingbirds. This Charleston, South Carolina garden is characteristic of those set-in tight spaces in old homestead cities like Savannah, New Orleans, Atlanta, and San Antonio.* (Artist's Retreat, Charleston, South Carolina. Photo by Mary Palmer Dargan)

*A front entrance is being used to feature plants that attract hummingbirds and butterflies. Ordinarily this would have been a boring turf-and-foundation planting.* (Rector, Baton Rouge)

*A container of plants that attract hummingbirds can be introduced for apartments and condominiums.* (Photo by Greg Grant)

ing plants to rather extensive developments, which include other traditional garden elements like paving, seating, water and other garden embellishments. The primary emphasis is on garden color and a rich assortment of plants which attract hummingbirds during their stay in the region. While cottage gardens have been famous in England and the European landscapes for centuries, the cottage garden look is only recently becoming quite popular in the United States. Plant outlets offer a huge assortment of flowering plants unheard of some ten years ago except to a few ardent gardeners who sought them out. With "color" plants being the major sales items in the cash and carry establishments as well as in the larger, more traditional plant nurseries, hummingbird plantings are becoming quite common as a part of the American garden scene. Such trends are surely different from the long-held tradition of planting heavy, permanent evergreens.

Many flower beds which are designed to attract hummingbirds may fall short of meeting the expectations of the artistic designer who carefully arranges plants in groups by color, form and texture in the proper compositional proportions. Gardens so frequently become a kaleidoscope of colors with the emphasis being on the ultimate performance of the plants which provide nectar for the birds. It is a relatively simple matter to grow a patch of horticulture specimens that provide food for hummingbirds. The challenge remains to design a garden with two major goals—to be an artistic composition expressive of sound design principles and at the same time to invite hummingbirds to the home grounds.

Herbaceous (annuals and perennials) plants are indeed the mainstay of the hummingbird garden. However, some woody plants normally should be added to provide a degree of permanence during the winter period when plants are dormant and the garden may appear somewhat neglected otherwise. Carefully selected woody specimens provide accent and anchor the more ephemeral, softer, flowering plants. In the South where growth is rampant, clipping and grooming plants within the composition is a continuing and necessary process to keep plants thrifty and producing an abundance of flowers throughout the summer and autumn months. Otherwise, plants become old and seedy and the more hardy ones are so competitive they crowd out their weaker neighbors.

Because these gardens rely heavily on annuals and perennials, they can be easily changed from year to year as you note whether some plants are more highly prized by hummingbirds than others. Even within a given year, more than one planting can be installed, since the growing season for much of the region is long and many annuals cannot be expected to perform at their best for extended periods.

*A garden designed for hummingbirds and butterflies have edges formed by cross ties and the path is covered with pine straw.* (Hope, Diamondhead, Mississippi)

*Public gardens, plant conservatories, and specialty gardens conduct important educational programs on plants and garden design. At the Biedenharn Gardens in Monroe, Louisiana, salvia, hibiscus, firebush* (Hamelia)*, and ixora are featured in this hummingbird planting.*

Hummingbird gardens need not be large. They can be modest parts of large developments. Most annuals and perennials attractive to hummingbirds need full sun and a fertile, well-drained soil. Close proximity to the house or other viewing areas where bird activity can be clearly seen is an important consideration. (An interesting part of the picture is viewing the wild array of air battles which take place among the birds defending territory.) It is unlikely that all the needs of hummingbirds can be supplied by flowers in a garden at any given time. Consequently, supplemental food provided in feeders is not only welcomed by the birds, but may be necessary to maintain large numbers of birds and their associated activities.

Following is a list of plants that may be used in landscape designs which also provide food for birds. It is understood that many other plants may fulfill landscapes needs that do not provide food for birds.

The letters following the common name refer to the area of the region to which the plants are best adapted. L = lower South, M = middle South and U = upper South.

## *Trees*

**Large—Deciduous**

| | |
|---|---|
| *Celtis laevigata* | Hackberry (LMU) |
| *Fagus grandifolia* | American Beech (LMU) |
| *Fraxinus pennsylvanica* | Green Ash (LMU) |
| *Liquidambar Styraciflua* | Sweet Gum (LMU) |
| *Liriodendron Tulipifera* | Tulip Tree (LMU) |
| *Quercus alba* | White Oak (LMU) |
| *Quercus falcata* | Southern Red Oak (LMU) |
| *Quercus falcata* 'pagodifolia' | Cherrybark Oak (LMU) |
| *Quercus michauxii* | Cow Oak (LMU) |
| *Quercus nigra* | Water Oak (LMU) |
| *Quercus Nuttallii* | Nuttall Oak (L) |
| *Quercus palustris* | Pin Oak (MU) |
| *Quercus phellos* | Willow Oak (LMU) |
| *Quercus stellata* | Post Oak (LMU) |
| *Sorbus Aucuparia* | European Mountain Ash (MU) |
| *Ulmus Americana* | American Elm (LMU) |

**Medium—Deciduous**

| | |
|---|---|
| *Acer negundo* | Box Elder (LMU) |
| *Albizia Julibrissin* | Mimosa (LM) |
| *Amelanchier arborea* | Serviceberry (LMU) |
| *Broussonetia papyrifera* | Paper Mulberry (LMU) |
| *Diospyros virginiana* | Common Persimmon (LMU) |
| *Maclura pomifera* | Osage Orange (LMU) |
| *Morus rubra* | Red Mulberry (LMU) |
| *Prunus serotina* | Black Cherry (LMU) |
| *Pyrus Calleryana* 'Bradford' | Bradford Flowering Pear (LMU) |
| *Sassafras albidum* | Sassafras (LMU) |
| *Sapium sebiferum* | Chinese Tallow Tree (LM) |
| *Sorbus americana* | American Mountain Ash (MU) |

**Small—Deciduous**

| | |
|---|---|
| *Aralia spinosa* | Devil's Walking Stick (LMU) |
| *Carpinus caroliniana* | Ironwood (LMU) |
| *Chionanthus virginicus* | Fringe Tree (LMU) |
| *Cornus Drummondii* | Rough-leaf Dogwood (LMU) |
| *Cornus florida* | Flowering Dogwood (LMU) |
| *Crataegus Marshallii* | Parsley Hawthorn (LM) |
| *Crataegus opaca* | Mayhaw (LM) |
| *Crataegus Phaenopyrum* | Washington Hawthorn (MU) |
| *Crataegus viridis* | Green Hawthorn (LMU) |
| *Disopyros Kaki* | Japanese Persimmon (LMU) |
| *Diospyros texana* | Texas Persimmon (Texas) |
| *Ficus carica* | Common Fig (L) |
| *Halesia diptera* | Silver-Bell (LMU) |
| *Ilex decidua* | Deciduous Holly (LMU) |
| *Malus angustifolia* | Southern Crab Apple (LMU) |
| *Malus floribunda* | Crab Apple (MU) |
| *Ostrya virginiana* | Hop Hornbeam (LMU) |
| *Prunus campanulata* | Taiwan Flowering Cherry (L) |
| *Prunus mexicana* | Mexican Plum (LMU) |
| *Prunus rivularis* | Hog Plum (LM) |
| *Rhamnus caroliniana* | Carolina Buckthorn (LMU) |
| *Rhus glabra* | Smooth Sumac (LMU) |
| *Sambucus canadensis* | Elderberry (LMU) |

**Evegreen—Large**

| | |
|---|---|
| *Magnolia grandiflora* | Southern Magnolia (L) |
| *Pinus echinata* | Shortleaf Pine (LMU) |
| *Pinus Elliotii* | Slash Pine (LM) |
| *Pinus glabra* | Spruce Pine (L) |
| *Pinus palustris* | Longleaf Pine (LM) |
| *Pinus Strobus* | White Pine (MU) |
| *Pinus Taeda* | Loblolly Pine (LM) |
| *Quercus virginiana* | Southern Live Oak (LMU) |

**Evergreen—Medium**

| | |
|---|---|
| *Cinnamomum camphora* | Camphor Tree (L) |
| *Ilex opaca* | American Holly (LMU) |
| *Juniperus silicicola* | Southern Red Cedar (LMU) |
| *Juniperus virginiana* | Eastern Red Cedar (LMU) |

**Evergreen—Small**

| | |
|---|---|
| *Calliandra hematocephala* | Red Powderpuff (L) |
| *Eriobotrya japonica* | Loquat (L) |
| *Erythrina crista-galli* | Coral Tree (L) |
| *Ilex Cassine* | Dahoon Holly (LM) |
| *Ilex cornuta* | Chinese Holly (LMU) |
| *Ilex cornuta* 'Burfordii' | Burford Chinese Holly (LMU) |
| *Ilex vomitoria* | Tree Yaupon (LMU) |
| *Ilex x attenuata* 'Fosteri' | Foster's Holly (LMU) |
| *Juniperus Ashei* | Ashe Juniper (LMU) |
| *Ligusturm japonicum* | Wax Leaf Ligusturm (LM) |
| *Ligustrum lucidum* | Tree Ligusturm (LMU) |
| *Myrica cerifera* | Southern Wax Myrtle (LMU) |
| *Myrica pennsylvanica* | Northern Bayberry (U) |
| *Podocarpus macrophyllus* | Japanese Yew (L) |
| *Prunus caroliniana* | Cherry Laurel (LMU) |

**Flowering Trees**

| | |
|---|---|
| *Acer rubrum* 'Drummondii' | Swamp Red Maple (LM) |
| *Amelanchier arborea* | Serviceberry (LMU) |
| *Albizia Julibrissin* | Mimosa (L) |
| *Calliandra haematocephala* | Red Powderpuff (L) |
| *Chionanthus virginicus* | Fringe Tree (LMU) |
| *Cornus florida* | Flowering Dogwood (LMU) |
| *Cartaegus Marshallii* | Parsley Hawthorn (LM) |
| *Crataegus Phaenopyrum* | Washington Hawthorn (MU) |
| *Crataegus opaca* | Mayhaw (LM) |
| *Crataegus viridis* | Green Hawthorn (LMU) |
| *Erythrina crista-galli* | Coral Tree (L) |
| *Halesia diptera* | Silver-Bell (LMU) |
| *Liriodendron Tulipifera* | Tulip Tree (LMU) |
| *Magnolia grandiflora* | Southern Magnolia (LM) |
| *Malus angustifolia* | Southern Crab Apple (LMU) |
| *Malus floribunda* | Crab Apple (MU) |
| *Prunus campanulata* | Taiwan Flowering Cherry (L) |
| *Pyrus calleryana* 'Bradford' | Bradford Flowering Pear (LMU) |
| *Viburnum rufidulum* | Southern Black Haw (LMU) |

## *Shrubs*

### Evergreen Shrubs

| | |
|---|---|
| *Abelia × grandiflora* | Glossy Abelia (LMU) |
| *Callistemon rigidus* | Bottlebrush (L) |
| *Clerodendrum paniculatum* | Pagoda Flower (L) |
| *Clerodendrum splendens* | Glory-Bower (L) |
| *Cotoneaster lactea* | Red Cluster-Berry Cotoneaster (MU) |
| *Elaeagnus multiflora* | Gumi (LM) |
| *Elaeagnus pungens* | Russian Olive (LMU) |
| *Fatsia japonica* | Fatsia (LM) |
| *Hibiscus rosa-sinensis* | Chinese Hibiscus (L) |
| *Ilex Cassine* | Cassine Holly (LMU) |
| *Ilex cornuta* | Chinese Holly (LMU) |
| *Ilex cornuta* 'Burfordii' | Burford Holly (LMU) |
| *Ilex glabra* | Inkberry (LMU) |
| *Ixora coccinea* | Ixora, or Flame-of-the-Woods (L) |
| *Ligustrum sinensis* | Chinese Privet (LMU) |
| *Lonicera fragrantissima* | Winter Honeysuckle (LMU) |
| *Mahonia Bealei* | Leatherleaf Mahonia (LMU) |
| *Nandina domestica* | Nandina (LMU) |
| *Photinia serrulata* | Chinese Photinia (LMU) |
| *Pyracantha coccinea* | Pyracantha (LMU) |
| *Russelia equisetiformis* | Fountain Plant (L) |

### Deciduous Shrubs

| | |
|---|---|
| *Aronia arbutifolia* | Red Chokeberry (LMU) |
| *Berberis Thunbergii* | Japanese Barberry (LMU) |
| *Callicarpa americana* | French Mulberry (LMU) |
| *Cotoneaster horizontalis* | Cotoneaster (MU) |
| *Euonymus americana* | Strawberry Bush, or Wahoo (LMU) |
| *Gaylussacia dumosa* | Huckleberry (LMU) |
| *Ilex ambigua* | Carolina, or Mountain, Holly (LMU) |
| *Ilex verticillata* | Winterberry (LMU) |
| *Lindera Benzoin* | Spicebush (LMU) |
| *Lonicera fragrantissima* | Winter Honeysuckle (LMU) |
| *Rosa species* | Garden Roses (LMU) |
| *Vaccinium arboreum* | Tree Huckleberry (LMU) |
| *Vaccinium species* | Blueberries (LMU) |
| *Viburnum dentatum* | Arrowwood (LMU) |

| | |
|---|---|
| *Viburnum Lentago* | Nannyberry (LMU) |
| *Viburnum Opulus* | Cranberry Bush (MU) |
| *Viburnum Wrightii* | Leatherleaf Viburnum (LMU) |
| *Weigelia florida* | Weigelia (LMU) |

**Flowering Shrubs**

| | |
|---|---|
| *Abelia × grandiflora* | Glossy Abelia (LMU) |
| *Aesculus Pavia* | Red Buckeye (LMU) |
| *Callistemon rigidus* | Bottlebrush (L) |
| *Clerodendrum splendens* | Glory-Bower (L) |
| *Hibiscus rosa-sinensis* | Chinese Hibiscus (L) |
| *Ixora coccinea* | Ixora, or Flame-of-the-Woods (L) |
| *Lonicera fragrantissima* | Winter Honeysuckle (LMU) |
| *Rosa* species | Garden Roses (LMU) |
| *Russelia equisetiformis* | Fountain Plant (L) |
| *Viburnum dentatum* | Arrowwood (LMU) |
| *Viburnum Lentago* | Nannyberry (LMU) |
| *Viburnum Opulus* | Cranberry Bush (MU) |
| *Viburnum Wrightii* | Leatherleaf Viburnum (LMU) |
| *Weigelia florida* | Weigelia (LMU) |

## *Vines*

| | |
|---|---|
| *Antigonon leptopus* | Coral Vine (L) |
| *Bignonia capreolata* | Cross Vine (LMU) |
| *Campsis radicans* | Trumpet Vine (LMU) |
| *Celastrus scandens* | Bittersweet (MU) |
| *Clerodendrum Thomsoniae* | Bleeding-Heart (L) |
| *Cocculus carolinus* | Carolina Snailseed (LMU) |
| *Gelsemium sempervirens* | Carolina Yellow Jessamine (LMU) |
| *Ipomea coccinea* | Red Morning Glory (LMU) |
| *Ipomea Quamoclit* | Cypress Vine (LMU) |
| *Lonicera japonica* | Japanese Honeysuckle (LMU) |
| *Lonicera sempervirens* | Coral Honeysuckle (LMU) |
| *Manettia cordifolia* | Firecracker Vine (L) |
| *Parthenocissus quinquefolia* | Virginia Creeper (LMU) |
| *Smilax* species | Southern Smilax (LMU) |
| *Vitis* species | Grapes (LMU) |

## *Perennials*

| | |
|---|---|
| *Clerodendrum speciossissium* | Java Plant (L) |
| *Cuphea ignea* | Cigar Flower (L) |
| *Cuphea micropetala* | Mexican Cigar Plant (L) |
| *Erythrina herbaceae* | Coralbean, or Mamou (L) |
| *Hamelia patens* | Firebush (L) |
| *Hedychium coronarium* | Butterfly Ginger (LM) |
| *Justicia Brandegeana* | Shrimp Plant (L) |
| *Justicia carnea* | Brazilian-Plume (L) |
| *Kniphofia Uvaria* | Red-Hot Poker (LMU) |
| *Lantana* species | Lantanas (L) |
| *Lobelia Cardinalis* | Cardinal Flower (LMU) |
| *Malvaviscus arboreus* | Giant Turk's Cap (L) |
| *Malvaviscus arboreus* 'Drummondii' | Turk's Cap (L) |
| *Monarda citriodora* | Lemon Mint, or Bee Balm (L) |
| *Odontonema strictum* | Fire Spike (L) |
| *Pentas lanceolata* | Pentas (L) |
| *Phytolacca americana* | Pokeberry (LMU) |
| *Salvia* species | Salvia (LMU) |
| *Spigelia marilandica* | Indian Pink (LMU) |

## *Annuals*

| | |
|---|---|
| *Helianthus angustifolia* | Swamp Sunflower, or Narrowleaved-Sunflower (LMU) |
| *Helianthus annuus* | Sunflower (LMU) |
| *Helianthus Maximiliani* | Maximilian Sunflower (LMU) |
| *Ipomea coccinea* | Red Morning Glory (LMU) |
| *Ipomea Quamoclit* | Cypress Vine (LMU) |
| *Salvia splendens* | Scarlet Sage (LMU) |
| *Tropaeolum majus* | Garden Nasturtium (LMU) |

*Northern Cardinal* (Cardinalis cardinalis) *by Murrell Butler*

# Birds in Southern Gardens

In the region covered by this book, there are over 375 species of birds, and approximately 70 species of these birds may be attracted to your Southern garden.

There are two categories of birds, permanent residents and migrants, that frequent Southern gardens. Permanent residents include such familiar species as Northern cardinal, Northern mockingbird, Eastern bluebird, American robin, Carolina chickadee, Carolina wren, and blue jay to name a few.

The migrants may be divided into three groups. First, those that come to the region for the winter, such as white-throated sparrow, cedar waxwing, hermit thrush, and purple finch. Second, birds that come from the more tropical regions of the Caribbean islands as well as Central and South America and breed in the region during spring and summer, include hummingbirds, orioles, summer tanager, indigo bunting, and purple martin. The third group are those that pass through the region twice yearly during migration, stopping for only a short period for feeding. These stay in the region for a period varying from a few days to a few weeks and include such species as bay-breasted warbler, gray-cheeked thrush, rose-breasted grosbeak, and scarlet tanager. The two tanagers may be summer residents of the more northern parts of the region.

Birds included in this book are those that feed on parts of plants that are useful as ornamentals in Southern home landscapes. Consequently, most of the insect feeders, like the flycatchers and warblers, are not included.

There are many outstanding books which are directed primarily towards identification, habitat, and behavior of birds only. The purpose of this book is to create a better understanding of plants which provide food, cover, or nesting sites for birds. This chapter focuses mainly on song birds that may be successfully attracted to Southern gardens.

Some birds will be found in all gardens, but the number of species and the level of activity are increased when the four basic needs for water, food, cover, and nesting sites are provided in the garden setting.

## *Pigeon Family*

**Mourning doves** (*Zenaida macroura*) are found year round in the region. They inhabit open woodlands, cultivated lands with scattered trees and shrubs, and arid areas of the western part of the region. Mourning doves are common in suburban gardens and frequently nest near human habitations. They may nest at least three times a year, often using the same nest and having no more than two chicks per brood. They are typically ground feeders, but will take millet and cracked corn from elevated feeders. They will also drink from watering stations in the garden. These doves are soft, sandy-buff colored with long, pointed tails bordered with white that is showy in flight. Their call, a low, mournful "*coo-ah, coo, coo, coo*" gives these doves their name. They are the only game bird in this book.

Plant food: Pine, pokeberry, millet, sunflower, and sweet gum.

## *Hummingbird Family*

**Hummingbirds** feed on the nectar of hundreds of species of cultivated and native plants. They are especially attracted to flowers that are tubular and red in color. They can be attracted to feeders when filled with a solution containing one part cane sugar and three to four parts water. Dissolve the sugar in boiling water, allow to cool, fill feeders and store unused portion in refrigerator until needed. Clean and refill feeders on a regular basis, allowing no more than five days between cleaning and refilling. Do not use honey, corn syrup, or artificial sweeteners in hummingbird feeders. Place the feeders in locations where they are in shade, away from the hot sunlight. Hummingbirds also need protein in their diet, which they obtain by eating tiny insects and spiders. One of our friends, who is an experienced birder, reports that hummingbirds feed on fruit flies that are attracted to over-ripened, partially peeled bananas. The bananas should be located close to a regular feeding station. In addition to the two species below, eleven other species of hummingbirds that breed in the western United States, Mexico, or the Caribbean have been recorded in the region.

*Mourning Dove*

**Black-chinned hummingbird** (*Archilochus alexandri*) is the most common hummingbird in much of Texas, breeding from the central part of the state westward. It is absent from the Panhandle and East Texas. The ruby-throated hummingbird is abundant there and they replace each other somewhere between Houston and San Antonio. Each winter, many black-chinned hummingbirds are found at feeders in East Texas and Louisiana, becoming much rarer farther east. The female has a whitish breast and throat and a green back, and in the field is virtually indistinguishable from the female ruby-throat. The male has a green back, black chin, and an iridescent violet band at the lower border of the black throat that is very difficult to see. It often nests along streams on a drooping limb of a willow or alder. It frequents semiarid chaparral canyons and foothills. It is found in suburban gardens with flowering plants. Five other species of hummingbirds breed in western Texas, and several others are visitors to the state.

**Ruby-throated hummingbird** (*Archilochus colubris*) is the smallest bird found in the region. It is the only hummingbird to breed in most of the region and has been reported to nest two or more times in a season. It is metallic green above and white below, and the male has an iridescent red throat (gorget). It spends winters in Central America and begins to arrive in the region in early March; it usually migrates south by late October. Each winter, a few are found at feeders along the Gulf Coast, but it is much scarcer than the rufous, black-chinned, and even the buff-bellied hummingbirds. It seems almost unbelievable that such a small bird could fly across the Gulf of Mexico, a distance of over 650 miles. It averages about thirty miles per hour, and at this rate it takes over twenty hours for them to make the trip. During the breeding season, it is found primarily in forested areas, but will visit suburban gardens if close to forest. During migration, it is much more common in the urban and suburban landscapes.

Flowering plants on which hummingbirds feed:

Excellent: Scarlet sage (including *S. coccinea* 'Lady in Red' and *S. splendens* 'Red Hot Sally'), Anise sage, Pineapple sage, firebush, flowering maple, and manettia.

Good: Mexican cigar, coral honeysuckle, 'Brazil' giant sage, 'Purple Majesty' sage, shrimp plant, trumpet vine, cardinal flower, lantana, Turk's cap, mimosa, bottlebrush, powderpuff, cross vine, pentas, red morning glory, ginger, Mexican sage, fountain plant, fire spike, and bleeding-heart vine.

Fair: Glossy abelia, Peruvian lily, red buckeye, rose of Montana, barberry, pagoda plant, coral tree, mamou, Carolina yellow jessamine, silverbell, Chinese hibiscus, cypress vine, Louisiana iris, nasturtium, red-hot poker plant, Japanese honeysuckle, honeysuckle bush, giant Turk's cap, azaleas, weigelia, horse mint, Indian pink, loquat, confederate jasmine, pagoda plant, yellow poplar, and others.

## *Woodpecker Family*

**Pileated woodpecker** (*Dryocopus pileatus*) is a year-round resident of the entire region, except West Texas. This crow-sized woodpecker is the largest seen in North America, other than the possibly extinct ivory-billed woodpecker. It prefers mature forests, but also seems to be adapting to second growth habitats and human encroachment, and is becoming fairly common in well-wooded suburbs. It nests in cavities in dead trees and snags. Carpenter ants in trees and stumps are its major food, and pairs often forage together. It has a solid black back, white neck stripes, and a large red crest.

Plant food: Common persimmon, pyracantha, sumac, American beech, black cherry, Virginia creeper, elderberry, and southern magnolia.

**Red-bellied woodpecker** (*Melanerpes carolinus*) is the most commonly seen of the region's woodpeckers. Habitats for this bird include deciduous woodlands, second growth, swamps, parks, and towns. It is easily attracted to the garden where it feeds on suet and mixtures containing peanut butter. The female brings her young to feeding stations to sample these treats. The male of these zebra-backed birds has a red crown and nape, but the female has red only on the nape. The hint of red on the belly is seldom seen under most field conditions. This and other woodpeckers consume vast numbers of wood-boring beetles, grasshoppers, ants, and other insects. The red-bellied woodpecker ascends trees in a jerky, curious fashion, and each move upward is accompanied by a hoarse "*chuh-chuh*." It is a food-storing bird, stashing away acorns and beechnuts. It nests in tree cavities and sometimes will nest in bird houses that have a floor cavity of four by four inches, with a twelve- to fifteen-inch depth of cavity, a two-inch entrance hole nine to twelve inches above the floor, and placed from twelve to twenty feet above the ground.

*Red-bellied Woodpecker*

Plant food: Maple, rough-leaf dogwood, flowering dogwood, gumi, common fig, sunflower, holly, crab apples, red mulberry, black gum, Virginia creeper, pokeberry, pines, black cherry, oaks, blackberry, dewberry, elderberry, American beech, smilax, American elm, grape, and blueberry.

**Red-headed woodpecker** (*Melanerpes erythrocephalus*) is a bird of the open, beech-oak woodlands and is also found locally in parks, cultivated areas, and rural and suburban gardens. This robin-sized bird is strikingly colored with the entire head red, wings and tail bluish black, white below, large white wing patch on each wing and a white rump. The white of the wing patch is very evident in flight. It is native to all parts of the region except southernmost Florida and West Texas. The red-headed and other woodpeckers nest in tree cavities, and its declining numbers in much of its range may be due to lack of nesting sites. Starlings often drive red-headed and other woodpeckers from nesting cavities they have labored to create. They do this not by force, but by making pests of themselves and harassing the woodpecker until it abandons its nesting site. The red-headed woodpecker likes suet, peanut butter mixtures, and will come to feeders for sunflower seeds. Bird boxes like those for the red-bellied woodpecker might attract this bird to your landscape.

Plant food: Rough-leaf dogwood, oaks, flowering dogwood, American beech, common fig, Southern magnolia, crab apples, red mulberry,

Red-headed Woodpecker

black gum, pokeberry, wild plum, pyracantha, sumac, rose, blackberry, dewberry, elderberry, Chinese tallow tree, sassafras, smilax, mountain ash, grape, and blueberry.

## Flycatcher Family

**Great crested flycatcher** (*Myiarchus crinitus*) is one of the few of the flycatcher family in the region to eat vegetation. It breeds throughout much of the region and then migrates to Central America and South America for winter. It occasionally winters in South Florida. It is found throughout the South the rest of the year. The great crested flycatcher is a mostly rural bird, inhabiting open forests and orchards, where it consumes large numbers of insects. It sometimes breeds in well-wooded suburbs. It uses shed snakeskins as lining for its tree-cavity nest, for reasons not understood. It is sometimes noisy, but seldom seen, as it lives in the forest canopy. This robin-sized bird is brown above, has a gray throat, yellow belly, rufous wings and tail, and is slightly crested.

Plant food: Virginia creeper, red mulberry, sassafras, black cherry, grape, spicebush, pokeberry, blackberry, blueberry, and rough-leaf dogwood.

**Eastern kingbird** (*Tyrannus tyrannus*), although chiefly an insect eater, frequents rural landscapes, where it occasionally feeds on fruits of several plants. It is an extremely skilled flier and can pluck berries from plants while on the wing. The Eastern kingbird is slightly smaller than a robin and is dull gray above and white below, with a white band on its blackish tail. A red crown patch is present, but seldom seen. It breeds through most of the region. It winters in South America, usually leaving by early October; its return begins in late March. It can often be seen sitting motionless on telephone wires and

*Great Crested Flycatcher* (Photo by Max Parker)

fences awaiting prey. The Eastern kingbird is extremely aggressive and will drive much larger birds, including some hawks and crows, away from its territory by dive-bombing the larger birds from above.

Plant food: Serviceberry, spicebush, Southern magnolia, black gum, Virginia creeper, pokeberry, blackberry, dewberry, elderberry, and sassafras.

## *Crow Family*

**Blue jay** (*Cyanocitta cristata*) is found throughout the entire South and, in winter some migrate to the region from farther north. Blue jays have a wide range of habitats, but prefer oak forests, open woodlands, parks, residential areas, and frequent suburban gardens. Their bright blue upper parts, white beneath and much white and black in the wings and tail make them eye-catchers. They have black facial markings and prominent crests. They are disliked by some because they are predators of eggs and young and may chase smaller species from feeders. However, their great beauty is a redeeming quality. Blue jays are reforestation agents in that seeds and acorns they bury are often not retrieved and so produce new plants. Pairs have been observed frequently at feeding stations eating sunflower seed, with one of the pair offering a seed to the other in apparent courtship behavior. Their most recognizable call, "*jay, jay, jay*," is part of a repertoire that includes imitations of the calls of red-shouldered and red-tailed hawks. Blue jays sound the alarm when a predator is near and their loud, raucous call rings out when they sight hawks or cats.

Plant food: Devil's walking stick, paper mulberry, fringe tree, camphor tree, flowering dogwood, parsley hawthorn, Japanese persimmon, Texas persimmon, common persimmon, gumi, loquat, American beech, fatsia, common fig, huckleberry, sunflower, holly, crab apples, red mulberry, black gum, pines, wild plum, black cherry, pyracantha, Bradford flowering pear, oaks, sumac, blackberry, dewberry, elderberry, Chinese tallow tree, and grape.

## *Swallow Family*

**Purple martin** (*Progne subis*) does not feed on plants, but is included here because it is easily attracted to landscapes that provide suitable nesting boxes. It is popular because of its gurgling notes, and its consumption of large numbers of insects. Human habitation and activities seem to have little effect on this highly social and communal swallow. It may be seen nesting in houses adjacent to busy shopping centers, service stations, and schools. The adult male is dark, purplish black, whereas the female is dull gray above and pale gray below. It is one of the first migrants to return from its winter quarters in South America, often arriving in late January or February. After nesting and raising young, the purple martin congregates in huge flocks and begins leaving by early August for its winter home. Sometimes as many as 250,000 purple martins gather at the south end of the bridge spanning Lake Pontchartrain near New Orleans and thousands of people come to observe them.

## *Titmouse Family*

**Carolina chickadee** (*Parus carolinensis*) is a permanent resident of the region, except in South Florida and West Texas. It is found throughout the region's forests, woodlands, and well-wooded suburbs. This small, tame bird can be easily identified by its repetitious call, "*chick-a-dee-dee*." Males and females have identical distinctive markings of a black cap and throat and a dull gray coat. The Carolina chickadee is fond of sunflower seeds and will come to feeding stations for them, most frequently in winter and then in small numbers. It is a cavity-nesting bird. To encourage more of the cavity-nesting birds, use a bird house that has a floor of four by four inches, with a ten-inch depth, a one-and-one-eighth-inch entrance hole six to eight inches above the floor, and the box placed six to fifteen feet above ground level.

Plant food: Maple, sunflower, sweet gum, pines, and American elm.

*This pair of Carolina Chickadees is cleaning out a knothole in a Chinese tallow tree for a nesting site. One is resting while the other is hard at work in the hole.*

*Tufted Titmouse*

**Tufted titmouse** (*Parus bicolor*) is a permanent resident of every state of the region. It inhabits forests, mesquite, parklands, and suburban areas, and frequently visits feeders. It is a crested bird, with upper parts and wings of mousy gray and under parts whitish with rusty flanks. The population in southwestern Texas has a darker crest and a small white forehead and was once considered to be a different species, called the black-crested titmouse. The song, a loud clear whistle, "*peter, peter, peter*," is often heard in the garden. This cavity-nesting bird can be attracted to the home grounds in wooded suburbs by erecting houses similar to those preferred by Carolina chickadee. Its range has expanded northward in the United States as a result of more feeders being stocked by gardeners and bird watchers, who supply them with sunflower seed.

Plant food: American beech, sunflower, crab apples, red mulberry, black gum, blackberry, dewberry, Virginia creeper, oaks, and grape.

## *Nuthatch Family*

**Brown-headed nuthatch** (*Sitta pusilla*) inhabits the pine forests and the pine-oak woodlands of the South. A dull brown crown, dull gray upper parts, and whitish underparts are some of its distinguishing characteristics. It feeds chiefly among the smaller, terminal branches. It is a very noisy species and is quite agile as it moves acrobatically from among clusters of pine needles and branches. This is not a bird likely to be found in many gardens and only comes to feeders located near its preferred pine habitat, and then mainly for black oil sunflower seed and possibly for suet.

 Plant food: Conifer seed and sunflower.

**Red-breasted nuthatch** (*Sitta canadensis*) breeds mainly in northern coniferous forests, but a few occur in the highest Appalachian Mountains. In winter it can be found over much of the region, but numbers vary dramatically from year to year. Red-breasted nuthatch prefers areas with some tall conifers, but is not as restricted to pines as is the brown-headed nuthatch. It is smaller than a sparrow, with upper parts gray and underparts pale rust. The male has a black crown. It has a white eyebrow and a black line through the eye. Called "the upside-down bird," it can be seen creeping downward, headfirst, on tree trunks in search of food. The seed of pine is its principal winter food. It occasionally will visit feeding stations to eat sunflower seed and suet.

 Plant food: Seed of conifers.

**White-breasted nuthatch** (*Sitta carolinensis*) is found in mixed deciduous-coniferous or pure deciduous forests and frequently in open woodlands, forest edges, and parks. It ranges over most of the region, but is absent from most of the Gulf Coast plain, South Florida, and West Texas. This nuthatch clings to tree bark and moves up and down in search of insects. It is fond of beechnuts, acorns, and pine seeds and visits feeders in winter for sunflower seed, peanut butter mixture, cracked corn, millet, and suet. The white-breasted nuthatch is a sparrow-sized bird, blue-gray above, with white underparts and face, and a black crown. Pairs generally remain in their home territories all year.

Plant food: Pin oak, sunflower, beech, and pines.

## *Wren Family*

**Carolina wren** (*Thryothorus ludovicianus*), the state bird of South Carolina is distributed throughout the South. Although this bird eats little vegetation, it is included because cozy nooks and corners about human homes seem to

*White-breasted Nuthatch*

be irresistible nesting sites for it. It will readily nest in wren houses, but if suitable nesting sites are not available it will nest in hanging baskets, tin cans, old hats, discarded boots or shoes and other things you would not dream it would use. It has been reported to build more than one nest before making a final choice. Bushy undergrowth of forests and woodlands is its favorite natural habitat, but it is common in wooded suburbs with adequate undergrowth. The Carolina wren is rusty brown above, buff below, with white on the throat and a whitish line over the eye. It gorges itself on mixtures containing peanut butter and also likes suet. It nests at least three times a year in part of the region.

Plant food: Sweet gum, osage orange, pine, and oak, all of which are insignificant in the diet.

*Carolina Wren. Mesh bags can be used for various mixes and nuts.*

## *Mimic Thrush Family*

**Gray catbird** (*Dumetella carolinensis*) breeds mainly in the northern half of the region, winters along the Gulf Coast in small numbers, and in greater numbers in Florida. It can be found in varied habitats, from hedgerows and gardens to thickets; dense, bushy areas; and undergrowth of the forest edge. The sexes of this mockingbird relative look alike, with a slender, long tail, dark gray plumage, with a black cap and rusty undertail coverts. Its most recognizable call is a catlike mewing, and thus its name "catbird." The gray catbird mimics the song of many other birds, and it is quite adept at imitating manmade sounds. It is a rural and suburban resident, but more frequently the former. Its well-concealed, twiggy nest, lined with finer plant materials, is often in dense brush. The gray catbird's diet is mostly insects, which makes it welcome in the garden, but it also eats fruits of many kinds of plants, some of which can be grown in almost any landscape.

*Gray Catbird* (Photo by C. Bernard Berry)

Plant foods: Serviceberry, parsley hawthorn, mayhaw, green hawthorn, Japanese persimmon, Texas persimmon, common persimmon, huckleberry, Ashe juniper, Eastern red cedar, crab apple, red mulberry, Northern bayberry, Southern

*Mockingbird eating fruit of common fig.*

wax myrtle, black gum, pokeberry, black cherry, pyracantha, Bradford flowering pear, Carolina buckthorn, sumac, rose, blackberry, dewberry, elderberry, spicebush, Virginia creeper, French mulberry, sassafras, smilax, grape, and blueberry.

**Northern mockingbird** (*Mimus polyglottos*) is the state bird of Texas, Arkansas, Tennessee, Mississippi, and Florida and is a permanent resident of the entire region. This slender, ten-inch long, long-tailed, gray bird with white patches on the wings and tail is known for its repertoire of songs. It is said that when windows are open on warm, spring, moonlit nights, its melodious tunes have caused mothers to think they had missed their alarm clock and arouse sleepy children from their abbreviated slumber to ready them for school. The mockingbird is extremely territorial and drives all others of its species from its turf. It is amusing to watch it defend food sources from such species as cedar waxwings, robins, cardinals, and others. It is successful against one or two invaders, but hoards of cedar waxwings swoop in on the guarded larder and often overwhelm the mockingbird's defenses. The mockingbird will also attack anything it considers a threat to its nest and young, including man, dogs, cats, and squirrels. Resident of both rural and urban areas, it seems to be one of the most successful bird species in adapting to city conditions. Two or more nestings a year have been reported, with each brood consisting of from three to five young. Although insects and animal matter constitute more than half its diet, the mockingbird feeds on a greater number of species of fruits than any other bird included in this book.

Plant food: Serviceberry, devil's walking stick, paper mulberry, bittersweet, fringetree, camphor tree, Carolina snailseed, rough-leaf dogwood, flowering dogwood, parsley hawthorn, mayhaw, green hawthorn, Japanese persimmon, Texas persimmon, common persimmon, Russian olive, gumi, Japanese plum, strawberry bush, fatsia, common fig, huckleberry, holly, Ashe juniper, Eastern red cedar, privet, honeysuckle bush, winter honeysuckle, Southern magnolia, Oregon grape, leatherleaf mahonia, crab apple, red mulberry, nandina, black gum, American hop hornbeam, Virginia creeper, Japanese yew,

*Mockingbird eating fruit of black cherry.*

photinia, pokeberry, wild plum, Taiwan cherry, cherry-laurel, black cherry, pyracantha, Bradford flowering pear, sumac, rose, blackberry, dewberry, elderberry, sassafras, smilax, mountain ash, tree huckleberry, grape, blueberry, Chinese tallow tree, and viburnum.

**Brown thrasher** (*Toxostoma rufum*), the state bird of Georgia, has one of the most beautiful voices of Southern birds, with a variety of musical phrases, each repeated twice. The song is similar to that of its relative, the Northern mockingbird. The brown thrasher is about the size of a blue jay with rufous-brown upper parts and white with dark brown streaks below. It usually forages on the ground and in thickets and woodland edges, and is at home below low-spreading shrubs in the landscape, where it searches for worms, insects, and seeds. In its search for food, it will pick up and move individual leaves and other debris. The brown thrasher is found in suburban and rural areas throughout the region. Bulky, twiggy nests are built in dense shrubs and trees; the Chinese privet is a favorite plant for nesting. More than one-half its yearly diet is from plant sources, and it favors juicy fruits. The brown thrasher can easily be attracted to feeding stations because it relishes suet in winter. It will eat mixtures containing equal parts of peanut butter, flour, cornmeal, and vegetable oil or lard at any time of the year. This bird is rather timid and is better observed at feeding stations from points that obscure the observer from its view.

Plant food: Serviceberry, devil's walking stick, red chokeberry, paper mulberry, flowering dogwood, rough-leaf dogwood, gumi, common fig, holly, juniper, cedar, Southern magnolia, red mulberry, Southern wax myrtle, Northern bayberry, black gum, Virginia creeper, pokeberry, pines, wild plum, black cherry, pyracantha, and blueberry.

*Brown Thrasher*

## True Thrush Family

**Eastern bluebird** (*Sialia sialis*) is one of the most beautiful and popular birds of the region and is primarily a bird of rural areas. Open farmlands, woodland edges, and woodlands composed of pine and oaks are prime habitats for bluebirds. The male is bright blue above, has a reddish brown breast, and is white below. The female has the same coloration, but is duller. The Eastern bluebird nests in cavities and has to compete with other birds seeking such nesting sites. A number of organizations have established bluebird trails, a series of nesting boxes spaced about one hundred yards apart, in many sections of the South. One of the longest stretches over one hundred miles along I-49 between Shreveport and Alexandria, Louisiana. Boxes along this trail are cardboard and most have to be replaced yearly. The Eastern bluebird can have two and, in some instances, three broods a year. It is not uncommon for the young of the first brood to help feed those of the subsequent broods of the year. Populations of Eastern bluebirds are greatest in winter, when birds from northern populations come South. Attract bluebirds by supplying nesting boxes, water, cover, and roosting boxes.

*Ruby-crowned Kinglet* (Photo by Charles Mills)

Plant food: Devil's walking stick, red chokeberry, bittersweet, camphor tree, Carolina snailseed, cotoneaster, rough-leaf dogwood, flowering dogwood, hackberry, Japanese persimmon, Texas persimmon, common persimmon, Russian olive, gumi, strawberry bush, huckleberry, holly, juniper, red cedar, privet, honeysuckle bush, Japanese honeysuckle, crab apple, red mulberry, Southern wax myrtle, Northern bayberry, black gum, Virginia creeper, pokeberry, Mexican plum, black cherry, pyracantha, sumac, rose, blackberry, dewberry, elderberry, sassafras, smilax, tree huckleberry, grapes, blueberry, and viburnum.

**Dark-eyed junco** (*Junco hyemalis*) breeds mostly in the far north and also in the Appalachian Mountains of the South. It winters throughout most of the region. It is scarce near the coast and most of Florida and Southern Texas, but is abundant in winter in Northwest Texas. This slate gray, white-bellied bird is about the size of a sparrow. The male is a darker gray than the female. White sides of the tail are conspicuous when the bird is in flight. The dark-eyed junco feeds mostly on the ground and can be enticed to the garden when millet is scattered in areas sparsely vegetated, yet near cover. The eastern populations of this bird were previously considered a separate species, the slate-colored junco. Its gray-and-blackish plumage blends well with dark soil and ground covers and makes it difficult to observe.

Plant food: Rose, millet, and sweet gum.

**Ruby-crowned kinglet** (*Regulus calendula*) is abundant in winter in wooded and brushy areas of the region, where it is often found in wooded suburban landscapes. This tiny bird, almost as small as a hummingbird, is olive gray above with white wing bars, and the male has a tuft of red feathers on the crown that is conspicuous only when excited. The kinglet is mostly insectivorous, flitting from tips of one branch to another seeking aphids, scales, and other tiny insects. It can occasionally be attracted to feeders with peanut butter mix and suet.

Plant food: Southern wax myrtle and Northern bayberry.

**American robin** (*Turdus migratorius*) is a permanent resident of all the region, although scarce in deep coastal South during nesting. Large populations are present in the region during winter, particularly when severe cold weather strikes the more northern areas. This ten-inch bird has a slate gray back and a red breast. The streaked throat, yellow bill, and white eye rings are distinct characteristics of the American robin. It inhabits both rural and urban areas and often can be found hopping on lawns, athletic fields, parks, and in open woodlands and fields.

Its cup-shaped nest is usually placed in the fork of a tree or shrub, but it will nest in special nesting shelves with overhead protection from rain. You may entice robins to nest in your garden by providing mud, which they use to line their nest. Earthworms are a favorite food, which it locates by sight and not by sound as many believe. It feeds on a number of fruits and one of its favorites is hackberry.

Plant food: Serviceberry, barberry, paper mulberry, French mulberry, bittersweet, hackberry, Carolina snailseed, cotoneaster, rough-leaf dogwood, flowering dogwood, Japanese persimmon, Texas persimmon, common persimmon, Russian olive, gumi, holly, Ashe juniper, Eastern red cedar, Japanese yew, privet, Southern magnolia, crab apples, red mulberry, black gum, Virginia creeper, photinia, pokeberry, wild plum, cherry laurel, black cherry, pyracantha, Bradford flowering pear, Carolina buckthorn, sumac, rose, blackberry, dewberry, elderberry, sassafras, smilax, Chinese tallow tree, and Virginia creeper.

**Gray-cheeked thrush** (*Catharus minimus*) is only seen in the area during migration in September and early October and from mid-April to mid-May. This bird has bold dark spots on a grayish breast, cheeks grayish, olive gray above, whitish below with olive gray on the sides. This thrush breeds in northern Canada and Alaska and winters in South America. During migration, it is found primarily in wooded areas; it is very difficult to observe.

*Gray-cheeked Thrush* (Photo by W. B. Lonnecker)

Plant food: Rough-leaf dogwood, flowering dogwood, spicebush, sassafras, black gum, black cherry, blackberry, dewberry, elderberry, smilax, sparkleberry, and grape.

*American Robin*

**Hermit thrush** (*Catharus guttatus*) migrates to the region in winter from more northern breeding areas; it arrives mainly after mid-October and is mostly gone by early April. It prefers forests and wooded areas with dense undergrowth. Insects and berries constitute its diet. It is reported that the hermit thrush likes the warmer river bottoms, but it is widely distributed in the region in winter. It is fairly common in wooded suburbs, but is rarely seen because it is shy and inconspicuous. It is olive brown above, with reddish tail, gray brown face, and thin whitish eye ring. It is whitish below with a pale cast and large spots on breast form narrow

*Veery* (Photo by Jacob Faust)

streaks on throat and flanks. It may be attracted to suet, peanut butter mix, or sliced apples.

Plant food: Serviceberry, hackberry, holly, juniper, Eastern red cedar, spicebush, Japanese honeysuckle, Virginia creeper, black cherry, pyracantha, sassafras, Carolina buckthorn, oaks, serviceberry, sumac, elderberry, sparkleberry, grape, and viburnum.

*Swainson's Thrush* (Photo by Jacob Faust)

**Swainson's thrush** (*Catharus ustulatus*) migrates through the region from mid-April to mid-May and from mid-September through October. It is found primarily in wooded areas. It is uniformly gray brown above and has a buffy eye ring and buff cheeks and upper breast. It is very similar to the gray-cheeked thrush, except for its buffy eye ring. Swainson's thrush sings during migration more often than other thrushes, making it more easily observable.

Plant food: Devil's walking stick, spicebush, barberry, hackberry, flowering dogwood, Russian olive, juniper, Eastern red cedar, red mulberry, Virginia creeper, pokeberry, black cherry, rose, blackberry, dewberry, elderberry, sassafras, smilax, and grape.

**Wood thrush** (*Hylocichla mustelina*) is a common nesting thrush in deciduous forests of the region. It has a bright rusty head, bold black spots on a white breast and white under parts, and the remainder of the body is rust colored. It is found in deciduous, secluded woodlands and in residential suburban and rural areas. Its flutelike carol in the quiet of the evening is considered by some to be one of our most beautiful bird songs. It migrates to Central America for winter. Wood thrushes mainly arrive in mid-April and leave by late October. It seldom visits feeding stations, but will take chopped prunes, raisins, and suet when placed in a sheltered, shady location.

Plant food: Devil's walking stick, barberry, French mulberry, cotoneaster, strawberry bush, spicebush, Southern magnolia, red mulberry, Virginia creeper, black cherry, pyracantha, Carolina buckthorn, sumac, rose, serviceberry, blackberry, dewberry, elderberry, sassafras, smilax, sparkleberry, and grape.

**Veery** (*Catharus fuscescens*) is one of the spotted-breasted thrushes and a resident of the mountains of the eastern part of the region and further north. Of all the brown thrushes, it has the least and most indistinct spots; its upperparts are a uniform orange-brown like those of the brown thrasher. Its range is extending southward. It migrates through most of the region to its winter range in South America. Preferring wetter habitats than other thrushes, it is found in dense, moist woodlands and stream-side thickets. It nests on or near the ground. The veery doesn't often leave the cover of its haunts near the ground and is infrequently seen, even in areas where common. Its eerie song is a blend of soprano and alto tones.

Plant food: Red mulberry, wild plum, mountain ash, spicebush, blueberry, black cherry, dogwood, elderberry, Virginia creeper, and serviceberry.

## *Waxwing Family*

**Cedar waxwing** (*Bombycilla cedrorum*) rarely breeds in the region; however, it winters here and can be seen in large flocks in late winter and spring. They fly in compact groups from one food plant to another and often strip every fruit from the plant before leaving it. It generally takes a flock of about one hundred birds four to five days to strip the fruit from three large 'Lord' hollies in our landscape. Favorite fruiting plants of these and other birds should not be planted in highway medians or roadsides because drafts of large vehicles will suck the birds down as they fly into the plants and cause them to be crushed and killed by oncoming traffic. Hundreds of cedar waxwings were killed on I-10 near New Orleans when they crossed the traffic lanes to reach pyracantha berries on plants in the median. The cedar waxwing is rich mauve brown, with a yellow belly and yellow tipped tail. Secondary wing feathers have tiny red structures on their tips. A velvety black line through the eye and black chin and forehead are distinguishing marks of this bird, and its crest lends further distinction to the cedar waxwing.

Plant food: Serviceberry, red chokeberry, barberry, bittersweet, hackberry, cotoneaster, flowering dogwood, Japanese persimmon, Texas persimmon, common persimmon, holly, Ashe juniper, Eastern red cedar, Japanese honeysuckle, Oregon grape, leatherleaf mahonia, red mulberry, black gum, pokeberry, Taiwan cherry, cherry-laurel, black cherry, pyracantha, Bradford flowering pear, Carolina buckthorn, blackberry, dewberry, elderberry, smilax, mountain ash, Indian hawthorn, Ardisia (Christmas berry), grape, and blueberry.

*Cedar Waxwing*

## *Starling Family*

**Starling** (*Sturnus vulgaris*) is a European import that takes over nesting sites from native birds which nest in cavities. (To prevent them nesting in bird boxes, make the entrance holes less than two inches in diameter.) Starlings were introduced in 1890 in an effort to provide North America with all the birds mentioned by Shakespeare, and this introduction was an overwhelming success. The one hundred birds released in Central Park in New York have spread over almost the entire nation. Many attempts have been undertaken to rid an area of these birds, but all have been unsuccessful. Starlings are rather shy birds, and so inexpensive food scattered on the ground far from feeding stations is one way of keeping them from areas where more desirable birds are fed. Starlings are scarce at feeders in the Deep South. A closer look at these birds will reveal that their iridescent purple and green feathers are whitish speckled.

Plant food: Paper mulberry, Virginia creeper, hackberry, camphor tree, flowering dogwood, common fig, privet, Southern magnolia, black gum, pokeberry, blueberry, Chinese tallow tree, and rough-leaf dogwood.

## *Vireo Family*

**Red-eyed vireo** (*Vireo olivaceus*) can be found throughout the region during the breeding season. In winter it migrates to South America, leaving by late October and returning in late March. It is abundant in deciduous woodlands and well-wooded suburbs. The upper parts, wings, and tail are olive green. The under parts are whitish and the crown is gray. The red eyes have whitish eyebrows and black eye line through each. The red eye is often difficult to see in the field. They build small cup-shaped nests in the forks of trees from five to forty feet above the ground. Their monotonous song is repeated from dawn to dusk and seems to be saying, "*Here I am, where are you?*"

Plant food: Serviceberry, spicebush, Southern magnolia, red mulberry, rough-leaf dogwood, Virginia creeper, black cherry, sumac, sassafras, and viburnum.

**White-eyed vireo** (*Vireo griseus*) is a common breeding resident of most of the region. This species prefers dense vegetation, such as second-growth thickets and forest edge. It is olive green above, white below, and has yellow flanks. It is much easier to hear than to see this secretive bird. The typical song is a loud, scolding, syncopated, five- to seven-note phrase, beginning and ending with a sharp "*chick*." The white-eyed vireo's song sounds like "*who are you, eh?*"

Plant food: Red mulberry, Southern wax myrtle, Northern bayberry, blackberry, dewberry, sassafras, grape, sumac, spicebush, flowering dogwood, and viburnum.

*Red-eyed Vireo* (Photo by C. Bernard Berry)

*Bay-breasted Warbler* (Photo by W. B. Lonnecker)

## Wood Warbler Family

**Yellow-breasted chat** (*Icteria virens*) inhabits areas of second growth, thickets, brushy areas, and fence-row vegetation. It breeds in all the South except South Florida. It winters in southern Florida, Texas, and to Central America. This large warbler has a yellow throat and breast, olive green above, white abdomen, and a black face mask bordered above and below with white. This bird, though widespread, is solitary, shy, and extremely difficult to see in its preferred habitat of dense vegetation. It has a bizarre collection of melodies and harsh sounds that are un-warbler-like. It has been reported that the yellow-breasted chat can often be heard at night from mid-April into October, but we've never heard it.

Plant food: Gumi, blackberry, dewberry, elderberry, blueberry, and grape.

**Bay-breasted warbler** (*Dendrocia castanea*) is one of the few warblers reported to use plant parts as food and then only from a small number. These rarely seen warblers are found in a variety of forests, woodlands, scrub, and thicket habitats, but only during migration. In our region, bay-breasted warblers are here primarily from late April to mid-May and again in October. In spring, males have chestnut sides, throat, and crown, and a buff patch in back of the head. They are greenish above and yellowish to whitish below, and are difficult to distinguish from other fall warblers, especially blackpoll and pine warblers. They nest mainly in Canada and migrate through the region to Central and South America.

Plant food: Red mulberry and Virginia creeper.

**Prothonotary warbler** (*Protonotaria citrea*) breeds in the entire region except western parts of Texas and Oklahoma, and winters in Central and South America. This warbler eats no vegetable matter, but is included in this book because it is easily attracted to gardens with nest boxes or water. It is not a shy bird and frequently

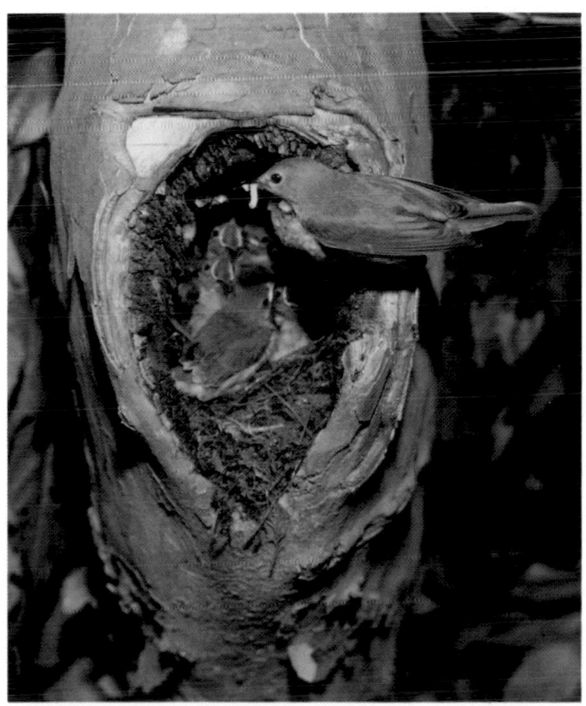

*Prothonotary Warbler* (Photo by Robert D. Buquoi)

*Yellow-rumped Warbler* (Photo by Max Parker)

nests in hanging plant baskets, bird boxes, and vertically standing tubes in carports or garages. The song of the prothonotary warbler is "*sweet, sweet, sweet, sweet, sweet*." The female is duller in appearance than the male, which is a golden bird with the entire head and breast a deep yellow-orange. There are no bars on the blue-gray wings. In the Catholic church, the prothonotary is the legal advisor to the pope and wears yellow vestments. The legal advice is so gentle as to be "sweet, sweet, sweet, sweet, sweet." This warbler is seldom found more than a few hundred yards from a body of water.

**Yellow-rumped warbler** (*Dendroica coronata*) winters in the South, leaving the region after mid-April for breeding grounds in northern Canada and Alaska. It is dull bluish above, with breast and flanks blackish and a yellow rump. The bright yellow side patches, prominent during the breeding season, are seen only briefly in the South. It is a widespread, abundant winter resident in almost all habitats, but especially near wax myrtles and bayberries.

Plant food: Flowering dogwood, Ashe juniper, Eastern red cedar, Virginia creeper, American beech, strawberry bush, Southern wax myrtle, Northern bayberry, pines, sumac, Chinese tallow tree, and American elm.

## *Weaver Finch Family*

**House sparrow** (*Passer domesticus*) was introduced in 1850 to help control cankerworms and is common throughout the United States near human habitation. The intended use for worm control was unsuccessful. The house sparrow's harsh, insistent "*chirp*" is the most common bird call heard in our villages, towns, and cities. It is an extremely common bird where people congregate for outdoor eating and picnics such as in parks and recreational areas. House sparrows are also abundant around feedlots. They will eat almost any type of food used in bird feeders and in large numbers they become a nuisance. Males are recognized by black bibs and bills with white cheeks; the plain, brownish females are often confused with other sparrows.

Plant food: Common fig, Japanese yew, American elm, sunflower, millet, and grape.

## *Blackbird Family*

**Red-winged blackbird** (*Agelaius phoeniceus*) inhabits bushes and small trees along water courses, upland cultivated fields, pastures, prairies, and fresh- and salt-water marshes. The male is black with bright red shoulder patches with yellowish margins. The female is brownish with well-defined dark stripes below. This blackbird is common in rice, millet, wheat, and other grain fields. The red-winged blackbird may be attracted to the garden with suet. It usually nests near water and raises two to three broods each year. It inhabits almost all of the United States. After the breeding season is over, red-winged blackbirds often congregate in huge flocks of hundreds of thousands that produce droppings at roosting places, which may create a health hazard.

Plant food: Millet, cracked corn, milo, and will eat suet.

**Brown-headed cowbird** (*Molothrus ater*) is famous as a brood parasite, laying its eggs in the nests of other birds which are generally smaller than themselves. Warblers, vireos, and sparrows are the most common host species, although brown-headed cowbirds lay their eggs in the nests of over two hundred species of host birds. The foster parents may abandon their nest, but generally they work tirelessly to incubate the parasites' eggs and to feed the young bird the food it needs. Because the host bird's young are usually much smaller, they suffer from the crowded conditions in the nest and do not get enough food to mature properly. The male cowbird is solid black except for a brown head. The female is gray without any distinguishing markings except for a dull, whitish throat.

 Plant food: Cracked corn and millet.

**Common grackle** (*Quiscalus quiscula*) is not a bird that most would like to attract to the garden. It is messy and brazen, and crowds smaller birds from feeders. This large, blackish bird often gathers with others in flocks of hundreds in late summer, fall, and winter. If it has redeeming qualities, they would be their beautiful eyes and the iridescent purple head of the male. The grackle may be partially discouraged by the use of small feeders such as those for finches, titmice, and chickadees. The common grackle breeds and winters in every state of the region.

Plant food: American beech, common fig, pine, black cherry, oak, blackberry, dewberry, elderberry, sunflower, and smilax.

**Northern oriole** (*Icterus galbula*) was formerly called Baltimore oriole and is one of the most vividly colored birds of the region. On males the breast, wing patches, and rump are fiery reddish orange, whereas the head, back wings, and tail are black. Females are olive-brown with dull yellow-orange underparts and two dull white wing bars. They breed over the entire region, but are less numerous in the coastal South. Their long, pendulous nest is built at deciduous woodland edges and shade trees twenty to thirty feet above ground, often over water. They are seldom found in highly populated areas, but may visit gardens where chopped or sliced fruits such as pears, apples, and orange halves are made available to them. They may also consume nectar from hummingbird feeders or drink it from special oriole feeders, which are large watering devices commonly used on poultry farms. They normally winter in Central and South America, but small numbers winter in the southern parts of the region. Most birds return in early April and leave by late September.

Plant food: Maple, serviceberry, common fig, crab apples, red mulberry, black cherry, Bradford flowering pear, oak, Carolina buckthorn, blackberry, elderberry, dewberry, mountain ash, American elm, grape, blueberry, and nectar from honeysuckles.

**Orchard oriole** (*Icterus spurius*) is smaller than the Northern oriole, and the male has a reddish brown breast and body with a black head, wings and tail. The female is yellow-green. It frequently nests in suburban areas. Its pendulous nest is similar to that of the Northern oriole in construction and is built on the tips of branches, often overhanging water. Ninety per cent of its diet consists of insects. It is attracted to feeders containing nectar made from sugar and water. This can be put in large watering devices like those used for Northern orioles. Be sure to place these in shaded areas to keep the contents relatively cool.

*Female Orchard Oriole perching by poultry waterer containing sugar solution.*

Plant food: Common fig, crab apples, black cherry, blackberry, dewberry, grape, red mulberry, and blueberry. Nectar from abutilon, cuphea, pineapple sage, iris, coral bean, Japanese and coral honeysuckles.

## *Tanager Family*

**Scarlet tanager** (*Piranga olivacea*) breeds in the upper South and winters in South America. The male is a beautiful scarlet with black wings and tail, and the female has greenish yellow upper parts and yellowish underparts. It spends most of its time high in tree tops and breeds in mature deciduous and mixed pine forests and occasionally in shade trees in rural and suburban areas. It will sometimes feed on the ground or at low feeders, but prefers platform feeders raised above the ground even at second-story window levels. It may be enticed to feeders supplied with slices of fresh fruit. Since it nests and feeds high above the ground, it is easily observable by high-rise apartment dwellers when the buildings are situated in a wooded area.

Plant food: Serviceberry, red mulberry, black cherry, blackberry, dewberry, sparkleberry, and grape.

**Summer tanager** (*Piranga rubra*) breeds over the entire area and winters mainly in Central and South America. A few birds are found in winter each year in the Gulf Coast states. The male is a uniform bright red, whereas the female and immature are yellowish to yellowish orange-brown with green tints to the wing coverts. It inhabits southern oak-pine forests, bottomland deciduous forests, and, in West Texas, willows and cottonwoods along streams. Like its close relative, the scarlet tanager, it is found in the upper branches of trees, especially during breeding. The summer tanager is not easily seen, but its presence may be easily detected by its unique call—a harsh, clear "*chicky-tucky-tuck*." It can be lured to feeding stations stocked with sliced fruit, with females being the most frequent visitors. Some wintering individuals feed on sunflower seed.

*Scarlet Tanager* (Photo by C. Bernard Berry)

*Summer Tanager* (Photo by C. Bernard Berry)

Plant food: Blackberry, black gum, black cherry, flowering dogwood, rough-leaf dogwood, gumi, elderberry, muscadine grape, red mulberry, and pokeberry.

## *Finch Family*

**Indigo bunting** (*Passerina cyanea*) is a migratory species that winters primarily in Central America, with a few wintering along the Gulf Coast. It breeds in all the region except West Texas and South Florida. The male is blue, whereas the female is a drab brown and paler beneath. This sparrow-sized bird is found in bushy pastures, overgrown fields, forest edges and in areas cropped with small grain, where it eats many insect pests and weed seeds. It spends much of its time foraging on the ground. Be alert for this bird when walking through grass or weedy and bushy pastures as you may flush the brown female from cover. The indigo bunting is a rural bird, but is known to frequent feeding stations in suburban settings during migration. Attract it with proso millet. As with many birds, Indigo buntings are attracted to water features, particularly moving water, in the landscape.

Plant food: Red mulberry, blackberry, dewberry, and elderberry.

**Painted bunting** (*Passerina ciris*) is probably the most strikingly colored bird occurring in the region. The male has bright red underparts and rump, green back, purple head, and red eye rings, whereas the female is one of the only true green birds of the region. The painted bunting is found in open situations with scattered trees and dense brush and weedy, grassy, scrubby, open

*Indigo buntings feed on proso millet when spread on the ground or in feeders. They may be present as singles or in large flocks.*

*Painted Bunting. This hand-held bird was banded for scientific studies.* (Photo by James V. Remsen, Jr.)

woodlands. It is reported to nest three times during the breeding season. This ground-feeding bird is not easily seen in the thick, often dense, growth of its habitat. The painted bunting infrequently comes to feeding stations for food. It ranges from northern Texas to southwestern Tennessee then south to the Gulf Coast, to central Florida. It winters in Florida, some of the Caribbean Islands, and Central America. The painted bunting feeds primarily on insects and grass seeds. Pools and birdbaths for bathing and drinking and proso millet and rice are the things most likely to attract it, and then only in rural areas.

 Plant food: Weed and grass seeds.

**Northern cardinal** (*Cardinalis*) is the state bird of Kentucky, Virginia, and Ohio. It is called "redbird" by most Southerners. A permanent resident of the region, the cardinal is adapted to a variety of habitats and is common around human habitation, in both urban and rural situations, bushy areas, fields, forests, and woodland edges. The male has a pointed crest and is bright red except for a black patch at the base of its stout, triangular bill. The female is buff-brown, with some red in the wing, breast, crest, and tail feathers. The Northern cardinal nests two or more times each year. It vigorously defends its territory during the breeding and nesting season, but is more tolerant of intruders during winter, particularly at feeding stations. This bird is popular at feeders, where it relishes sunflower seed, with the black oil preferred. It feeds on seeds and fruits of many plants.

Plant food: Maple, devil's walking stick, paper mulberry, French mulberry, ironwood, bittersweet, hackberry, fringetree, camphor tree, flowering dogwood, hawthorn, gumi, fatsia, common fig, ash, huckleberry, sunflower, firebush, lantana, privet, sweet gum, Southern magnolia, red mulberry, American hop hornbeam, pokeberry, pine, black cherry, pyracantha, sumac, rose, blackberry, and dewberry.

**House finch** (*Carpodacus mexicanus*) is a native bird of the western United States that has spread nearly nationwide since caged birds were released in the 1940s in New Jersey. It is often mistaken for the purple finch; however, it is smaller and the male is more orange-red and has dark stripes on the sides of the belly. The female is brown, having a white underside with dark stripes. It may be distinguished from the female of the purple finch in that it has a smaller bill and no dark cheek patch or heavy mustache. In the region, this finch is found primarily in the suburbs and in agricultural areas with shrubs and trees. It frequents feeders stocked with sunflower seed. House finches are reported to offer stiff competition for house sparrows at feeders and may even discourage them from taking over feeding stations.

Plant food: Wild sunflower, sunflower, and pine.

**Purple finch** (*Carpodacus purpureus*), a small, sparrow-sized bird, is a winter visitor to the region. Numbers present and the depth of penetration into the region vary from year to year. They spend the winter in flocks and are frequent visitors to feeding stations stocked with black sunflower and thistle seed. Males have rosy-red, almost raspberry, coloration on their heads and rumps, whereas females and immature birds are brownish with pronounced striping on their breasts. In size and color, the females and immature may be confused with sparrows or pine siskins. Purple finches are primarily birds of the woodlands and forest edge, but are easily attracted to suburban landscapes where there are moving water, berrying plants, and well-stocked feeders.

Plant food: Maple, cotoneaster, American beech, Ashe juniper, Eastern red cedar, privet, osage orange, crab apples, red mulberry, black gum, American hop hornbeam, Virginia creeper, pine, pyracantha, Bradford flowering pear, sumac, American elm, grape, and viburnum.

**American goldfinch** (*Carduelis tristis*) is a winter resident of the entire region, including most of southern Florida. It breeds in the northern part of the Gulf states into Canada. In winter the males and females are a dull yellowish gray, have black wings with white wing bars, and black tails. In winter it is difficult to distinguish males from females, but the males have blacker wings and more yellow on the head. Males begin molting as early as mid-January and become a bright yellow with white rump, white edges on black wings and tail, and black forehead. Flocks of more than a hundred birds are not unusual. Goldfinches are not shy birds and can be found in significant numbers even in urban gardens. They will be persistent guests of your home grounds when supplied with feeders stocked with thistle (niger), their favorite, or black oil sunflower seed. They are late nesters and often remain in the southern range of their winter quarters until early May. Nesting is often delayed until midsummer. Like many seed-eating birds, they inhabit cultivated and weedy fields, shrubby second-growth areas, open woodlands, and forest edges.

Plant food: White ash, box elder, American elm, American hop hornbeam, grape, sunflower, rose, red mulberry, osage orange, pines (loblolly, shortleaf, slash), serviceberry, sweet gum, and thistle.

*Purple Finch* (Photo by C. Bernard Berry)

**Blue grosbeak** (*Guiraca caerulea*) is slightly smaller than a cardinal and is a breeding resident in most of the region except West Texas and South Florida. It winters in Central America, but a few birds are found each winter near the Gulf Coast. This ground-feeding bird frequents shrubby thickets, weedy pastures, and stream edges lined with tall, weedy vegetation. It will occasionally visit rural home grounds where millet or other seeds have been scattered in grass areas. Both sexes of these small finches have two

*American Goldfinch*

*Rose-breasted Grosbeak*

buff wing bars and large dark bills. Males are dark blue and females dark buff-brown. They gather in flocks in fall to forage in milo and millet fields in search of seeds and insects. They may sit motionless for a considerable period of time and easily escape detection.

Plant food: Wild sunflower, sunflower, blackberry, and dewberry.

**Evening grosbeak** (*Coccothraustes vespertinus*), a chunky, eight-inch-long member of the finch family, is a resident of northern coniferous forests and the mountainous areas of the region. Evening grosbeaks move south during winter, but it is rare that they can be found in great numbers in the Deep South. Only every six or seven years are there appreciable numbers in the lower South, for reasons not clearly understood, but probably related to scarcity of food. Males have brown heads, shading to yellow on the lower back, rumps and underparts; and have short, black tails and black and white wings. Females and immature males are streaked gray-brown, have yellow rumps and white spots on the tail. Sunflower seed is a favorite of evening grosbeaks, and they sometimes gather in small flocks of up to several hundred about feeding stations or in tree tops. In winter, their food supply is almost entirely from plant sources. Evening grosbeaks are not related to the other two grosbeaks—they only share a "grosbeak" name because of their large bills.

Plant food: Maple, ironwood, flowering dogwood, parsley hawthorn, green hawthorn, ash, sunflower, Ashe juniper, Eastern red cedar, sweet gum, coral honeysuckle, osage orange, crab apples, and American elm.

**Rose-breasted grosbeak** (*Pheucticus ludovicianus*) breeds only in the mountainous areas of the South and in central Oklahoma. It winters in Central and South America and can be seen for short periods in most of the region during its migrations. A few winter each year in the Gulf Coast region, often at feeders. It inhabits deciduous forests and woodlands. Coloration is very different in the sexes, with the male being black-and-white with a conspicuous rose red patch on the breast and underwings. The female has prominent white eyebrows and is white above and below, heavily streaked with brown. It may nest near human habitation in wooded towns and suburbs. It occasionally pauses at feeding stations on its migration routes to feed on sunflower seed.

Plant food: Barberry, flowering dogwood, American beech, sunflower, wild sunflower, red mulberry, sweet gum, American hop hornbeam, Virginia creeper, black cherry, oaks, blackberry, dewberry, elderberry, and viburnum.

**Pine siskin** (*Carduelis spinus*) is found in the region in winter but only during very severe, cold weather is it found in great numbers in the coastal South. This bird of diminutive size has a brownish, heavily streaked body, lighter on the underparts, with yellow patches on the base of the outer tail feathers and in the wings. The yellow in the wings and tail is not always evident. The male and female have the same coloration. It may travel in flocks of a hundred or more and will monopolize feeders stocked with thistle and sunflower seed. It is found in open fields, farmlands, woodland edges, and may be common in suburban landscapes.

Plant food: Maple, pine, sunflower, sweet gum, and American elm.

**Chipping sparrow** (*Spizella passerina*) is a summer resident of all the region except the southernmost parts. In winter it is present from the middle South into Mexico. This small sparrow has a reddish brown cap and brown-streaked upper parts with whitish gray underside. Its habitat includes woodlands and garden edges, open meadows and thickets, and shrubby areas near woodlands. In winter virtually one hundred percent of its food is seeds taken on the ground. Millet and cracked corn attracts it to the garden. The song is by no means a musical happening, as it is a monotonous "*chippy-chippy-chippy-chippy*," giving this bird its name.

*Chipping Sparrow* (Photo by W. B. Lonnecker)

*Pine Siskin* (Photo by Jacob Faust)

Plant food: Juniper, cedar, pecan, and elderberry.

**Fox sparrow** (*Passerella iliaca*) is found in the region only during the winter and is scarce near the Gulf Coast. The most concentrated populations are along rivers. It has a reddish rump and tail with a reddish triangular marking on the breast. The foxy look of this sparrow is produced by the rust and gray coloration about the neck. This ground feeder scratches among fallen leaves mainly for seeds and this scratching behavior is so automatic that it practices it even at feeders.

Plant food: Strawberry bush, Ashe juniper, Eastern red cedar, Virginia creeper, blackberry, dewberry, elderberry, smilax, and grape.

**Song sparrow** (*Melospiza melodia*) is a permanent resident of the upper South and in winter is found in the entire region. It has a dark central

*Song Sparrow* (Photo by W. J. Turnbull)

breast spot on white underparts heavily streaked with brown. It is welcome in the garden for its bright, cheerful song. It sings every month of the year, even in foul weather, and is reported to sing at night. About ninety percent of its winter

*White-throated Sparrow*

diet is seeds and it can be attracted with millet and cracked corn. Prefers woodland edges, weedy fields, and pond margins where there is thick brush for cover.

Plant food: Rose, millet, Virginia pine, and elderberry.

**White-throated sparrow** (*Zonotrichia albicollis*) is a ground-feeding sparrow present in the region only during winter. In winter it likes dense, bushy growth with a semi-open canopy. Ninety per cent of the diet is vegetable matter, mainly seeds and small fruits. It has a well-defined white throat, yellow spot above and in front of the eye, two wing bars, a plain gray breast, and notched tail. Some say its Deep South vocalization is "O *Acadia-Acadia-Acadia*," whereas farther north it is said to sing pure sweet "*Canada-Canada-Canada*," and those with no regional inclinations say it says "*O Sam peabody-peabody-peabody*." It seldom comes to raised feeders, but will eat proso millet and cracked corn scattered on the ground.

Plant food: American beech, millet, wild sunflower, spicebush, sweet gum, pines, smilax, and viburnum.

**Rufous-sided towhee** (*Pipilo erythrophthalmus*) is a permanent resident of most of the region. Its annual diet consists of 70 percent vegetable materials, with large amounts of acorns being eaten in winter. Rufous-sided towhee is primarily a ground feeder, but it may be enticed to feeding stations with seed during winter. The male of this large, long-tailed bird has a black hood, white wing patches, white tip of tail, and the sides are rufous, thus its name. The female is virtually identical, but has a brown head. As the towhee feeds, it scratches noisily with both feet. It has a distinctive song, "*drink-your-tea*," by which it easily identified.

*Rufous-sided Towhee*

Plant food: French mulberry, huckleberry, sunflower, holly, sweet gum, Oregon grape, leatherleaf mahonia, crab apples, red mulberry, Northern bayberry, Southern wax myrtle, pines, black cherry, oaks, blackberry, dewberry, elderberry, sassafras, millet, tree huckleberry, and grape.

Other species that may be attracted to the home grounds are **downy and hairy woodpeckers,** which visit suet feeders and feed on some garden fruits. While these woodpeckers are not as showy as the others discussed here, they may be frequently seen in the landscape.

**Yellow-bellied sapsucker** is noted for drilling holes in trunks of trees and large shrubs to encourage sap flow on which it feeds. It feeds on fruit and is present in wooded suburbs. It is ubiquitous, but so quiet that it isn't seen often.

**House wren** is a common nester in the northern part of the region and likes garden wren houses.

**Solitary vireos** winter in suburbs in Gulf Coast states and eat the fruit of garden plants.

**Orange-crowned warbler** winters in suburbs near the coast and sometimes visits hummingbird feeders.

**Harris' sparrow** is common during winter in north central Texas and Oklahoma. It comes to feeders for proso millet and sunflower seed and will also feed on these when spread on the ground close to cover.

**Field sparrow** visits feeders in rural areas in winter.

**Swamp sparrow** winters in the region and will sometimes visit feeders in rural areas.

**Pine warbler** will visit suet feeders in winter.

A recent survey conducted by the Mississippi Department of Wildlife, Fisheries and Parks indicates that the top ten favorite backyard birds are:

1. Northern cardinal
2. Carolina chickadee
3. Tufted titmouse
4. American goldfinch
5. Ruby-throated hummingbird
6. Eastern bluebird and blue jay (tie)
7. Carolina wren
8. Mourning dove
9. Northern mockingbird and purple finch (tie)
10. Red-bellied and red-headed woodpeckers (tie)

*American Goldfinch* (Carduelis tristis) *by H. Douglas Pratt*

# Plants for Southern Gardens

Habitat loss due to increases in farm operations, highway and airport construction, expanding suburbia, various kinds of pollution, and human disturbances have threatened or endangered many animal and plant species.

Foresters report that more trees exist now than were present seventy to eighty years ago. However, large scale clear-cutting of the woodlands and subsequent reforestation with a single species does not restore the original ecosystem, where biological diversity provided habitat for birds and wildlife. Recent reports indicate that some forests do not revert back to their state existing prior to clear-cutting and even partial recovery may take as much as a century. During this period, clear-cutting of the trees may be done two or more times, depending on the type of agroforest operation. Large tracts of land planted in pines, as practiced in much of the South, results in a habitat suitable for few birds and other wildlife.

Prior to World War II, farming operations in the South were smaller, with many individual farms planted with a wider crop diversity. Instead of one or two crops, several crops were generally grown and there were also livestock operations on a limited scale associated with most of these small farms. The greater variety of crops and grazing land provided better wildlife habitat than exists today, where thousands of acres are devoted to only one or two crops. In addition, the use of a multitude of pesticides has become a common farming practice. Most of these are applied by airplane and the coverage by this method allows few birds in the coverage area to escape without being contaminated by the pesticide. Drift of the materials can occur when the materials are not properly applied and can contaminate nesting and feeding areas in nearby hedgerows and woodlands.

The construction of the interstate highway system destroyed millions of acres of woodlands. However, some good resulted from this construction. Many trees adjacent to the highway rights-of-way were killed or damaged and died over a period of time. These damaged or dead trees provided excellent nesting sites for woodpeckers and other cavity nesting birds that followed them. The clearings for the highways also allowed the regrowth of plants along the margins, providing an excellent edge effect so desirable for bird habitat.

Most migratory birds, including those that winter in Central and South America, require relatively large forest areas for successful breeding. Even though the total acreage of woodlands has increased in recent years through reforestation and government assistance programs, the areas available for good wildlife habitat have not increased proportionally. This imbalance is due to the construction of roads, housing developments, shopping centers, airports, and recreational areas that fragment large woodland tracts. Small woodlands are dangerous places for songbirds to breed for several reasons. First, many of the migrant birds are too small to defend their territory and nest from larger predators, such as crows, grackles, and jays, which eat both their eggs and young. Eggs and young are also more vulnerable to cats, dogs, opossums, skunks, and raccoons, which are more numerous in pocket-sized habitats. Many of the predators are not associated with large tracts of heavily wooded forest. The brown-headed cowbird is a considerable threat to successful breeding of many songbirds. This small fringe-dwelling bird tricks other species into rearing its young by depositing its eggs in the nest of other birds. It sometimes ejects the eggs of the host bird. Cowbird nestlings hatch early, grow quickly, and are formidable competitors for the food supplied by the host parents. Songbird populations have been devastated in parts of the Midwest by cowbird predation.

The gardener living in a rural, suburban, or urban area has an opportunity to increase and conserve wildlife and plant populations and at the same time provide habitats for wildlife, especially for birds, by selecting and planting those plants that are threatened. In the South a great variety of plant materials is available that fill landscape needs as well as provide the variety in sizes and kinds that attract birds. To create a diverse habitat, intermingle plants of different sizes, shapes, and textures to fulfill your landscape needs. Variety in plants gives birds a choice of food—seed, nuts, fruits, berries, flower nectar, and supplies nesting sites and cover. Insects, worms, and spiders that are attracted to plants are important for most birds, especially those that are feeding young.

Unfortunately many common ornamental trees, shrubs, vines, and ground covers are of little value to birds. Also, many of these plants are the standard ones of the nursery trade which are not endangered and need the least help for conservation. Even where there are existing plants in the landscape, enrichment with threatened or endangered native plants and others providing food and shelter for birds can make for interesting and functional landscapes.

Planning is the most important step in landscaping the home grounds. The needs of the family—space for shade, flowers, fruit, work areas, outdoor recreation—and wildlife habitat are some of the important considerations that enter into making landscape decisions. Plants are the basic building blocks for our landscape developments. In choosing a plant, consider its ultimate size, maintenance requirements, susceptibility to insect and disease pests, as well as its aesthetic qualities. The maintenance of landscape plantings can have a significant impact on energy and water consumption and on the environment. Those that require frequent fertilization, watering, spraying, pruning, and winter protection should be used in minimal numbers or avoided where other more trouble-free plants will satisfy the landscape need. Good stewardship of our environment demands that we use less fertilizer, water, and pesticides in maintaining our home grounds.

Plants providing some of our most colorful flowers, fruits, and berries are highly attractive to birds. Vines, shrubs, and trees that fulfill aesthetic and functional needs in our home grounds are also important for cover or nesting sites for birds. In choosing plants for bird attraction, consider the kinds of birds you want to frequent your garden and then select plants that fulfill their habitat requirements. If you want birds in your landscape the entire year, you should consider not only the resident birds but also those that are migrants into the region. This means that you will need plants that supply food and shelter for most of the year, and it is only through planning that this goal can be achieved. Properly selected plants can provide habitat and food for birds throughout the year, particularly in winter when supplies of food sources and insects are in limited supply.

An article in *Natural History* by Edward N. Stiles gives four factors that normally affect a bird's choice of food. These include fruit or seed size, amount of lipids (fats), amount of sugars, and length of time the fruit stays on the plant.

Even larger birds such as American robins and mockingbirds usually do not consume fruits over three-fifths of an inch in diameter. While an American robin can easily eat the fruit of a cherry laurel, a much smaller cedar waxwing could only eat parts of the fruit after it has been mechanically crushed into smaller pieces.

Fruits high in lipids or fats generally ripen in the fall at the time birds migrate. Birds need this high-fat diet to supply them with the energy for their long flights. Fruit high in lipids include that of the spicebush, flowering dogwood, hackberry, black-oil sunflower, sassafras, and magnolia. However, fruits high in fats do not last long, as fungi and bacteria quickly avail themselves to this food source and cause them to decay rather quickly.

Fruit and seeds high in sugar content generally ripen in spring and summer, at the time of year when protein-rich insects are plentiful and are needed by birds for raising young. Among the most common high-sugar fruits are blackberries, dewberries, mulberries, cherries, huckleberries, loquats, and elderberries. Even in winter, the high-sugar-containing fruits may be passed over when high-lipid-containing fruits, nuts, and insects are available.

In the South many plants retain their fruits and berries until late winter and into spring. When there is an abundance of fruit, it is not uncommon for many plants to hold their fruits and shed them naturally after new growth begins in spring. Examples of plants which retain their fruits are many hollies, ligustrums, cherry laurel, some viburnums, sumac, smilax, pyracantha, and nandina.

Regionally adapted plants that provide good bird habitats as well as fulfill landscape needs are discussed in this chapter. The zones to which they are adapted refer solely to cold hardiness. Cold hardiness zones were based on information contained in the *USDA Plant Hardiness Zone*

*Map* (Agricultural Research Service, Miscellaneous Publication Number 1475, January 1990).

Winter survival of landscape plants is probably the most critical factor in their adaptation to the environment. Such factors as soil fertility, drainage, acidity or alkalinity of the soil, sun or shade requirements, moisture requirements, and maintenance requirements greatly influence growth and must be understood. It is possible to overcome some of the factors that could limit a plant's performance in your garden by correcting the growth-limiting factors to near optimum levels. For example, soils that are too acid may be amended with lime to bring them to the proper pH level for satisfactory growth of particular plants. Where rainfall is limited, supplemental water can be supplied and grade changes can be made to facilitate drainage. These conditions must be studied during the planning stage and the needed adjustments made prior to planting. However, the best solution may be to select those plants that will grow best under the conditions that you have in your garden. For more information on these and other plant problems, contact your local County Cooperative Extension Office.

Landscape so that you can see the bird-attracting features from a convenient window, indoor living area, patio, or terrace. With careful planning, selection, planting, and maintenance you can have a succession of flowers, foliage, fruits, and nuts that both you and the birds can enjoy.

The following descriptions provides basic information on plants which are most frequently used for attracting birds to landscapes in the region.

# Trees

*Acer Negundo* **BOX ELDER**
**Family:** *Aceraceae* Deciduous Tree
**Zone:** 4a
**Fruiting:** Autumn
**Size:** 30' × 20'

This fast growing, eastern, native tree is normally a volunteer in moist flood plain soils. It grows in full sun to partial shade. Having three to five leaflets, it is one of the few maples with a compound leaf. The main bird attraction are the v-shaped, winged paired seeds that mature in late autumn.

**Birds:** Purple finch, evening grosbeak, pine siskin, cardinal, American goldfinch, Carolina chickadee, red-bellied woodpecker, rose-breasted grosbeak, and song sparrow.

**Comments:** Other maple seeds eaten by birds include: red maple, silver maple, sugar maple, swamp red maple, and Norway maple.

**Box elder.** *Seed of this and other maples used by birds.*

**Mimosa.** *An outstanding source of nectar for hummingbirds. Occasionally one can find hummingbirds hanging from the tree, assumed to be intoxicated on fermented nectar.*

*Albizia Julibrissin* **MIMOSA**
**Family:** *Leguminosae* Deciduous Tree
**Zone:** 8a
**Flowering:** Late spring
**Size:** 35' × 35'

Once a highly visible and popular tree which had naturalized over most of the region, the mimosa population has decreased due to a soil-borne fungus disease, mimosa wilt. Even though the disease is present, mimosas are still fairly common. This broad-spreading tree grows in a wide range of acid to alkaline, moist to dry soils and tolerates sea coast conditions. The fluffy heads of powder-pink flowers attract hummingbirds in great profusion.

**Birds:** Hummingbirds.

**Comments:** When mimosa is in flower, it is a preferred food source favored over most other flowering plants and birds make fewer feeding visits.

**Serviceberry.** *Performs best in upper South.*

*Amelanchier arborea* **SERVICEBERRY**
**Family:** *Rosaceae* Deciduous Tree
**Zone:** 3b
**Flowering:** Midspring
**Size:** 25' × 10'

This native large shrub to small tree has a wide distribution over the eastern United States. It grows best in slightly acid soils with a high organic matter content and adapts well to relatively dry to moist conditions. Growing best as an understory species, it will tolerate full sunlight. White, fragrant flowers are borne in racemes three to seven inches across before the foliage in spring. Foliage color in autumn is outstanding in hues of orange and red. Birds are attracted to the red-purple, applelike fruits which are present in early to midsummer.

**Birds:** Eastern kingbird, gray catbird, mockingbird, brown thrasher, Northern oriole, American robin, scarlet tanager, hermit thrush, wood thrush, red-eyed vireo, veery, pileated woodpecker, red-winged blackbird, and cedar waxwing.

**Comments:** Serviceberry is especially well adapted to plantings along ponds, rivers, streams, and on damp, wooded slopes.

*Aralia spinosa* **DEVILS'S-WALKING STICK**
**Family:** *Araliaceae* Deciduous Tree
**Zone:** 6a
**Fruiting:** Early autumn
**Size:** 20'–30' × 8' (clumps)

This plant is normally associated with woodland edges and grows in colonies which become very large if left undisturbed. It is usually a single-trunked, unbranched, heavily thorned, stout trunked tree. Devil's walking stick grows in fertile, acid soils with high humus component. Excellent for naturalistic plantings, it will grow in full sunlight to partial shade. In late summer, small white flowers appear in clusters up to four feet long. Flowering is followed by prominent clusters of bright, shiny purple, berrylike fruit which ripen in autumn.

**Birds:** Cardinal, mockingbird, brown thrasher, blue jay, gray catbird, wood thrush, Swainson's thrush, and Eastern bluebird.

**Comments:** Makes an excellent intermediate sized fruiting plant for naturalistic landscape plantings and woodland edges.

**Devil's walking stick.** *Gets its name from the heavily spiny stems. Birds clean the fruit, leaving showy, purplish red stems.*

**Paper mulberry.** *Only female plants produce fruit, which resembles "Medusa's" head, with the orange, fleshy seeds protruding from the green ball.*

*Broussonetia papyrifera* **PAPER MULBERRY**
Deciduous Tree
**Family:** *Moraceae*
**Zone:** 6a
**Fruiting:** Early summer
**Size:** 25'–40' × 30'

Not a true mulberry, this dioecious (male and female flowers on separate plants) tree was introduced from Asia for the purpose of making paper and tapa cloth. Because it grows in a wide range of soil types and produces an abundance of seeds and suckers and reseeds itself so profusely, this tree sometimes becomes a nuisance in well-maintained landscapes. The many orange seeded drupelets protrude from a marble-sized receptacle in summer.

**Birds:** Mockingbird, starling, cardinal, brown thrasher, American robin, and blue jay.

**Comments:** Both male and female plants must be present for fruiting to occur. Volunteers may be male or female, thus it is possible to have large colonies of non-fruiting plants. It is reported that the fruit of the paper mulberry is sweeter and more tasty than the red mulberry (*Morus rubra*).

*Calliandra haematocephala* **RED POWDERPUFF**
Tropical Evergreen Tree
**Family:** *Leguminosae*
**Zone:** 9b
**Flowering:** Year-round
**Size:** 10' × 16'

A tropical tree with characteristics similar to mimosa, produces two-inch, red, powderpufflike flowers and has a limited range for outdoor use. It is especially well adapted as a container grown specimen during the warm months in other parts of the region where it is given winter protection from frost. Use it very much like you would Chinese hibiscus. Provide full sunlight and a well-drained, fertile soil.

**Birds:** Hummingbirds.

**Comments:** Makes an excellent, large tub specimen for viewing hummingbirds at close range. Suited for outdoor culture only in South Florida and the citrus growing area of Texas.

**Red powderpuff.** *A flower atop emerging foliage.*

*Carpinus caroliniana* **IRONWOOD**
**Family:** *Betulaceae* Deciduous Tree
**Zone:** 3b
**Fruiting:** Summer and autumn
**Size:** 30' × 25'

This native understory species is found growing near fresh water streams in deep, rich, moist sites normally associated with other hardwoods such as beech, elm, and hornbeam. It grows slowly in sunlight to partial shade. Adding or removing soil from around this tree will nearly always result in its death. The fruit is a nutlet attached to a three-lobed wing arranged in drooping clusters which turn brown in autumn.

**Birds:** Cardinal, American goldfinch, and evening grosbeak.

**Comments:** Ironwood is seldom available in the nursery trade and is difficult to transplant, especially in large sizes.

**Ironwood.** *A more prevalent tree today than in colonial days because cutting it was such a difficult task.*

*Celtis laevigata* **HACKBERRY**
**Family:** *Ulmaceae* Deciduous Tree
**Zone:** 5a
**Fruiting:** Autumn
**Size:** 50' × 40'

A native found over the entire eastern United States, this fast-growing tree is adapted to most soils from very poor to fertile and acid to alkaline. Highly drought tolerant, it grows well under the stressful conditions of center cities. Hackberry fruits are small, cream-colored nuts to about one-fourth inch in diameter. The hackberry has dependable yellow autumn foliage color. Hackberry is an early succession tree and provides needed shelter in coastal areas for migratory birds as they make their way from Central and South America to the United States in spring.

**Hackberry.** *Among the best bird foods.*

**Birds:** American robin, Eastern bluebird, cardinal, mockingbird, starling, cedar waxwing, Swainson's and hermit thrushes.

**Comments:** Because of the litter associated with the tiny twigs and its highly competitive root system, the hackberry is best adapted for open lawn areas.

*Chionanthus virginicus* **FRINGE TREE**
**Family:** *Oleaceae* Deciduous Tree
**Zone:** 6a
**Fruiting:** Late summer
**Size:** 20' × 12'

A native large shrub to small tree, it has a profusion of white fringelike flowers in spring and small olive-shaped, dark blue fruit in summer. Best performance is in full sunlight to partial shade as an understory tree beneath tall-growing pines. It must have a slightly acid, well-drained soil. The large leaves, up to six inches in length, turn yellow in autumn.

**Birds:** Mockingbird, blue jay, pileated woodpecker, and cardinal.

**Comments:** There are male and female plants, with the male producing the most showy flowers. The literature reports only one bird species eating the fruit, but recent observations of fruits on plants growing in open areas have shown that this is a good food for several birds. The fruit, produced on older wood is somewhat obscured by the foliage produced on current seasons growth.

**Fringe tree.** *Fruit being enjoyed by an immature cardinal.*

**Camphor tree.** *Go for cover when this fruit is ripe, because bird droppings are plentiful.*

*Cinnamomum Camphora* **CAMPHOR TREE**
Evergreen Tree
**Family:** *Lauraceae*
**Zone:** 8b
**Fruiting:** Fall
**Size:** 60' × 40'

This fast-growing Oriental tree is relatively sensitive to cold. When it is subjected to periodic freezes, top growth is killed back to the main trunk and sometimes to the ground. For this reason, few people realize that when mature, this tree has a loose, open form similar to a live oak. It thrives in most soils, but prefers a moist, fertile, loam soil in full sunlight to partial shade. The two-inch glossy leaves are highly aromatic and when crushed, give off a camphor odor. The fruit is a black drupe about the size of a large pea.

**Birds:** Mockingbird, cardinal, Eastern bluebird, blue jay, American robin, and starling.

**Comments:** Large populations of the camphor have volunteered in the urban areas of the lower South, since seeds are widely dispersed by birds. Populations are cyclic due to periodic freezes every 15 to 20 years. Camphors and trees with similar soft, fleshy fruits should not be planted in close proximity to buildings, walks, outdoor living areas, parking areas, and drives because of fruit stains and bird droppings.

*Cornus Drummondii* **ROUGH-LEAF DOGWOOD**
**Family:** *Cornaceae* Deciduous Tree
**Zone:** 5a
**Fruiting:** Autumn
**Size:** 20' × 15'

A native, deciduous tree that is widely distributed over the entire South in huge populations growing in soils which are heavy and wet to those that are moderately dry. It is usually seen growing along woodland edges but will grow in full sunlight to shade as an understory species where fruiting is sparse. Volunteers can be expected to appear nearly everywhere due to dispersal by birds. In spring it produces clusters of small, white flowers which are less showy than the native flowering dogwood. White berries, which are somewhat less showy than the native flowering dogwood, are prominent in autumn after the foliage drops.

***Rough-leaf dogwood.*** *Fruit ripens very early, in midsummer, and the white fruits are particularly showy from a distance.*

***Flowering dogwood.*** *Flower, foliage, and fruit make this among the most beloved small trees in the region.*

**Birds:** Eastern bluebird, cardinal, evening grosbeak, mockingbird, American robin, gray-cheeked thrush, red-headed woodpecker, red-bellied woodpecker, brown thrasher, red-eyed vireo, Acadian flycatcher, summer tanager, and Eastern kingbird.

**Comments:** Relatively short-lived tree that is easy to grow. Premature defoliation due to a leaf fungus disease is common. A tree worthy of much greater acceptance for areas with stressful conditions where other small deciduous trees will not grow.

*Cornus florida* **FLOWERING DOGWOOD**
**Family:** *Cornaceae* Deciduous Tree
**Zone:** 6a
**Fruiting:** Autumn
**Size:** 25'–30' × 20'

Undoubtedly, the dogwood is the most popular native flowering tree in the region. Dogwoods produce white "flowers" (actually bracts) in spring, pleasant summer foliage canopy, beautiful autumn foliage, and clusters of showy red berries in autumn. It is a highly temperamental tree which requires a loose, moist, well-drained, acid soil. Provide partial shade for dogwoods, but they can be grown in full sunlight when growing conditions are ideal. Dogwoods will not tolerate heavy, poorly drained soils. Primarily grown for its flowers, the autumn color and red fruit are added attractions and fruits are high in lipid or fat content.

**Birds:** Eastern bluebird, cardinal, blue jay, American robin, red-headed woodpecker, evening grosbeak, mockingbird, starling, summer tanager, brown thrasher, gray-cheeked and Swainson's thrushes, cedar waxwing, rose-breasted grosbeak, and yellow-rumped warbler.

**Comments:** Dogwoods generally do not flower for several years after planting. In selecting planting sites for dogwoods, best results are obtained when the planting area is on the south to southeast side of a building receiving morning sun and afternoon shade where the soils are well-drained. It is difficult to predict their performance. Colors range from white to deep pink to almost red. The Chinese dogwood, *Cornus Kousa* 'Chinensis,' is adapted to the upper South and produces large white flowers followed by red, strawberrylike fruit.

*Crataegus Marshallii* **PARSLEY HAWTHORN**
Deciduous Tree
**Family:** *Rosaceae*
**Zone:** 7a
**Fruiting:** Autumn
**Size:** 20' × 15'

This small, native, eastern U.S. tree with its parsleylike foliage is well adapted to a wide range of soil conditions. It tolerates alkaline to acid soils, even those which are poorly drained. Growth is best in well-drained soils in full sunlight to high shade. The showy white flowers in spring are followed by clusters of small applelike berries in October and are particularly showy after leaf drop.

***Parsley hawthorn.*** *Among best of hawthorns for bird food.*

**Comments:** Fruits seldom persist for long periods during the fall because they are highly prized as bird food. Young, immature trees produce thorns one or more inches long that may be hazardous. An added attraction in old trees is the open, sculptural form of the trunks.

*Crataegus Phaenopyrum* **WASHINGTON HAWTHORN**
Deciduous Tree
**Family:** *Rosaceae*
**Zone:** 5b
**Fruiting:** Autumn
**Size:** 25' × 20'

This spring-flowering tree ordinarily produces prominent, white flowers with pale yellow anthers in late April or May. It has a sensational display of bright red, lustrous, quarter-inch fruit in autumn. Its upright, dense habit, profuse flowers and brilliant color of foliage in autumn as well as its showy fruits are assets that few other trees possess. It grows best in well-drained, slightly acid soils, but will tolerate a wide range of soil conditions. Prefers full sunlight and grows

**Washington hawthorn.** *This species has outstanding fruit in the middle and upper South.*

**Mayhaw.** *People try to get this fruit before it is eaten by wildlife.*

well in partial shade. It is best adapted to upland soils out of the coastal plains.

**Comments:** A selection of this species, Pyramidal Washington Hawthorn (C. *Phaenopyrum* 'fastigata'), has a columnar growth habit and fewer and smaller flowers and fruit.

*Crataegus viridis* **GREEN HAWTHORN**
**Family:** *Rosaceae* Deciduous Tree
**Zone:** 5b
**Fruiting:** Autumn
**Size:** 35' × 20'

This is the largest growing and most widely distributed hawthorn native to all parts of the South. Well adapted to moderately heavy soils, it grows best in full sunlight or as a weak understory specimen. Clusters of white flowers in spring are followed by small applelike fruit in autumn and these persist through late winter.

**Comments:** The mayhaw (C. *opaca*) has large flowers appearing in late winter followed by fruits one or more inches in diameter and is highly prized for jelly-making. In every part of the region there is at least one or more species of hawthorn that can be successfully grown.

**Birds that feed on hawthorns:** Cardinal, blue jay, mockingbird, evening grosbeak, brown thrasher, and gray catbird.

**Green hawthorn.** *The fruit of this hawthorn is eaten only after the supply of other preferred fruits has been depleted.*

*Diospyros Kaki* **JAPANESE PERSIMMON**

**Family:** *Ebenaceae* Deciduous Tree

**Zone:** 7b

**Fruiting:** Autumn

**Size:** 20' × 12'

This popular fruiting tree introduced from the Orient produces large, rounded, four-inch orange to reddish fruits that are prominent after the leaves drop. Requiring full sunlight and a fertile, well-drained soil, the Japanese persimmon produces no seeds to a very few, so it must be propagated by grafting.

**Comments:** This widely grown ornamental and fruiting tree is prized by many for its uniquely flavored fruit. Many species of wildlife find the fruit equally attractive and may consume the fruits before they can be harvested for human consumption.

***Texas persimmon (trunk).*** *Noted for its striking, peeling bark.* (Photo by Benny Simpson)

***Oriental persimmon.*** *This fruit is large enough to provide food for many birds.*

*Diospyros texana* **TEXAS PERSIMMON**

**Family:** *Ebenaceae* Deciduous Tree

**Zone:** 7a

**Fruiting:** Autumn

**Size:** 40' × 25'

This native Texas persimmon is grown primarily in Texas and is somewhat smaller than the common persimmon. It is well adapted to well-drained limestone soils. Small black, dark-fleshed fruits, approximately one inch in diameter are abundant in fall. White, peeling bark is an attraction throughout the year.

**Comments:** Both male and female trees are required for pollination and fruit set. This highly drought tolerant species can be used as an understory tree and as singles or massed in a tight grove arrangement to feature its interesting trunks.

***Texas persimmon (fruit).*** *This persimmon fruit has an unusual purplish black color when it is ripe.* (Photo by Benny J. Simpson)

**Common persimmon.** *Eaten by many species of birds.*

*Diospyros virginiana* **COMMON PERSIMMON**
Deciduous Tree
**Family:** *Ebenaceae*
**Zone:** 4b
**Fruiting:** Autumn
**Size:** 50' × 25'

A widely distributed native tree found along the edges of woodlands, open fields and fence rows, it is tolerant of most soil conditions from wet to dry in full sunlight. Persimmons are among the earliest species to appear in noncultivated lands. The prominent yellow-orange fruit are very astringent until they fully ripen following the first frost. An additional feature is the striking yellow to red autumn foliage which drops relatively early, exposing the bright orange fruits.

**Comments:** Both male and female plants must be present for fruit to be produced. This species suckers freely, forming clonal colonies of varying sized trees.

**Birds that feed on persimmons:** Mockingbird, blue jay, American robin, gray catbird, pileated woodpecker, Eastern bluebird, and cedar waxwing.

*Eriobotrya japonica* **JAPANESE PLUM or LOQUAT**
Evergreen Tree
**Family:** *Rosaceae*
**Zone:** 8a
**Fruiting:** Spring
**Size:** 25' × 20'

A highly prized fruiting tree in its native Orient, this somewhat tender evergreen tree prefers full sunlight and a loose, fertile, well-drained, slightly acid to alkaline soil. One of the few, coarse-textured, evergreen trees which can be used in small spaces. The winter bloom provides nectar for hummingbirds which migrate from western areas of the United States to the Coastal South. The yellow-colored, edible fruit, one or more inches in diameter, matures in early spring.

**Birds:** Blue jay, mockingbird, and hummingbirds on nectar.

**Comments:** Highly susceptible to fireblight disease which normally affect its longevity. Cannot be expected to fruit in its northern limit of growth, since freezes destroy the flowers and developing young fruit in winter.

**Loquat or Japanese plum.** *Winter flowering and spring fruiting.*

*Erythrina crista-galli* **CORAL TREE**
**Family:** *Leguminosae* Deciduous Tree
**Zone:** 8a
**Flowering:** Spring and summer
**Size:** 20' × 15'

Coral tree tolerates harsh environmental conditions. It is a semitropical plant that thrives in full sun and well-drained soils, but will grow in many soil types. Is often seen in old established center-city neighborhoods where it normally receives some cold protection. The form can range from a single-trunked tree to a broad-spreading, multi-stemmed, shrublike plant. Large, loose, prominent spikes of tubular, crimson flowers extend beyond the foliage. Under ideal conditions, as many as 30 or more two inch florets are borne on each flowering stalk.

**Birds:** Hummingbirds.

**Comments:** A profuse producer of nectar which drips from the flowers in the form of a tear drop, thus giving it another common name, the "cry-baby" plant. Highly subject to freeze injury in most parts of the region except for the lower coastal zones.

**Coral tree or crybaby tree.** *This fast-growing plant produces flowers with an abundant supply of nectar.*

**American beech.** *Woodpeckers store the nuts.*

*Fagus grandifolia* **AMERICAN BEECH**
**Family:** *Fagaceae* Deciduous Tree
**Zone:** 4a
**Fruiting:** Autumn
**Size:** 100' × 70'

Among America's most highly prized shade trees, the beech can be found growing in well-drained, acid, fertile soils. Normally associated with woodland conditions, it is a long-lived species. The three-angled nuts, which are enclosed in a prickly husk opening in autumn, are eaten by a large number of wildlife. The light, silver-colored, thin bark and retention of brown leaves in winter are other distinguishing features.

**Birds:** Evening and rose-breasted grosbeaks, blue jay, white-breasted nuthatch, white-throated sparrow, red-bellied and red-headed woodpeckers, tufted titmouse, purple finch, and common grackle.

**Comments:** The beech is extremely sensitive to construction operations that affect grade changes, soil compaction and water table alterations. It is poorly adapted to stressful environments.

**Common fig and young cardinal.** *Rise early to beat the birds to this delicious fruit.*

*Ficus carica* **COMMON FIG**
**Family:** *Moraceae* Deciduous Tree
**Zone:** 7b
**Fruiting:** Midsummer
**Size:** 15' × 20'

A highly prized fruiting tree in the lower South, it grows best in moist, fertile, well-drained soils that have a relatively high humus content. Figs produce fruit best in full sunlight, but will perform satisfactorily in partial shade. Trees planted in the upper limits of its growing range will be killed back periodically and three to five years are required before significant fruit is produced again. The outstanding characteristics are its coarse textured foliage, multistemmed form and delicious fruit, which may be eaten fresh or preserved.

**Birds:** Cardinal, mockingbird, brown thrasher, red-headed and red-bellied woodpeckers, blue jay, starling, house sparrow, and Northern and orchard orioles.

**Comments:** Many cultivars are grown in the South, but the most dependable and popular is 'Celeste.' Other selections grown in the region include 'Brown Turkey,' 'Magnolia,' and 'Florentine.' References seldom list fig fruits as a bird food, but nearly all fruit-eating birds present at the time of ripening will feed freely on figs.

*Fraxinus pennsylvanica* **GREEN ASH**
**Family:** *Oleaceae* Deciduous Tree
**Zone:** 4a
**Fruiting:** Autumn
**Size:** 60' × 40'

A native tree widely distributed over most of the eastern United States, the green ash grows best in fertile, moist soils, and full sunlight. It also tolerates relatively heavy, poorly drained soils in river flood plains. Having a medium-fast rate of growth, it is among our most dependable shade trees and provides brilliant yellow autumn color.

**Birds:** Cardinal, evening grosbeak, purple finch, and red-winged blackbird.

**Comments:** Other ashes that attract birds are the white ash (*F. americana*), which seems to be more prevalent in the upper South and the Arizona ash (*F. velutina*), which performs relatively well in the drier parts of the region, but is a short-lived, messy tree in the lower South.

**Green ash.** *Fruits are showy for several months in the green state before they ripen and are eaten by birds in autumn and winter.*

*Halesia diptera* **SILVER-BELL**
**Family:** *Styracaceae* Deciduous Tree
**Zone:** 7b
**Flowering:** Spring
**Size:** 30' × 25'

A native tree that is widely distributed along sandy streams with well-drained, slightly acid soils. Silver-bell grows well in full sunlight to partial shade and has a medium rate of growth. The white, bell-shaped flowers appear in clusters of three to six flowers and hang below the emerging foliage. In addition to the spring flowers, other features include the oval shaped, thin leaves to three inches across and the striking yellow autumn color.

**Birds:** Hummingbirds.

**Comments:** Silver-bell is an excellent substitute for flowering dogwood in areas which have relatively heavy, poorly drained soils. It makes a superb patio shade tree. A close relative, the Carolina silver-bell, (*H. carolina)* should be used in the upper range of the region.

***Silver-bell.*** *Among the best adapted and most underutilized of the medium-sized flowering trees.*

***Ozark white cedar or Ashe juniper.*** *The fruit of this juniper is reported to have a sweet flavor and is eaten by a large number of birds in its native western habitat.* (Photo by Benny J. Simpson)

*Juniperus Ashei* **WHITE CEDAR, ASHE JUNIPER**
**Family:** *Cupressaceae* Evergreen Tree
**Zone:** 7a
**Fruiting:** Autumn
**Size:** 20' × 15'

This native juniper is well adapted to harsh environments with full sunlight and poor, thin, alkaline limestone soils of the western parts of the region. Both male and female plants are required for the production of the blue, glaucous, quarter-inch fruits. The fragrance of the cut foliages is an added feature.

**Comments:** This juniper is relatively fast growing under dry, adverse conditions, making it useful for mass screening and naturalistic plantings. It is resistant to cedar-apple rust, a disease which attacks many other junipers.

*Juniperus silicicola* **SOUTHERN RED CEDAR**
**Family:** *Cupressaceae* Evergreen Tree
**Zone:** 7a
**Fruiting:** Autumn
**Size:** 30' to 40'

This is the principal tree on Cedar Key, Florida, the site of John Muir's famous Florida walking trip. At this location it is much smaller than in more sheltered locations. It fruits heavily and differs from the Eastern red cedar in having more slender twigs, smaller female cones and larger male catkins.

**Eastern red cedar.** *The berries of this juniper are used to flavor gin as well as being a major bird food.*

*Juniperus virginiana* **EASTERN RED CEDAR**
**Family:** *Cupressaceae* Evergreen Tree
**Zone:** 3b
**Fruiting:** Summer and autumn
**Size:** 30'–40' × 30'

A long-lived, widely distributed, native juniper which grows well in poor, thin, well-drained, alkaline soils and full sunlight. It is relatively slow growing except for those cultivated in good garden soils. The picturesque form develops after a specimen is 25 or more years old. The bluish, berrylike fruit up to one-fourth inch in diameter is present on female plants only in fall and winter.

**Comments:** It has a moderate degree of salt tolerance, thus making it a valuable evergreen for plantings near the coast. It is subject to attack by cedar-apple rust and bagworms. Other selections which have been introduced for landscape uses include: 'Canaertii,' 'Glauca,' 'Burkii,' and 'Cupressifolia.'

**Birds that feed on junipers:** Mockingbird, Eastern bluebird, American robin, cedar waxwing, evening grosbeak, brown thrasher, gray catbird, hermit thrush, Swainson's thrush, yellow-rumped warbler, purple finch, chipping sparrow, and fox sparrow.

*Liquidambar Styraciflua* **SWEET GUM**
**Family:** *Hamamelidaceae* Deciduous Tree
**Zone:** 6a
**Fruiting:** Autumn
**Size:** 100' × 60'

Sweet gum is a dominant species of the region volunteering freely in moist, fertile, slightly acid, alluvial soils, but tolerant of most growing conditions. It grows relatively fast for the first 15 years. Noted for its autumn color, usually maroon, but sometimes yellow and red, the sweet gum is one of the most dependable for fall color in the lower

**Sweet gum.** *Many ground-feeding birds relish the small seeds as they are shed from the gum balls.*

South. Male and female flowers appear on the same plant. The male is catkinlike and the female has the characteristic spiny head which eventually forms the encasement for the small, black seeds that are released in autumn.

**Birds:** Cardinal, mourning dove, purple finch, American goldfinch, dark-eyed junco, evening grosbeak, pine siskin, Carolina chickadee, rufous-sided towhee, and white-throated sparrow.

**Comments:** The persistent, hard, spiny sweet gum balls are a nuisance in highly manicured gardens.

*Liriodendron Tulipifera* **TULIP TREE**
**Family:** *Magnoliaceae* Deciduous Tree
**Zone:** 5b
**Flowering:** Spring
**Fruiting:** Autumn
**Size:** 150' × 60'

Among the tallest and most widely distributed natives in the region, this excellent shade and timber tree grows best in moist, fertile, sightly acid to neutral soils. It must have good drainage and is absent from the flood plains. On mature trees, tulip-shaped, two-inch-long flowers with greenish yellow petals marked with orange, are somewhat concealed by spring foliage. The yellow autumn leaves fall and expose an abundance of two-to three-inch, cone-shaped, many seeded pods.

**Birds:** Hummingbirds feed on the nectar and the evening grosbeak eats the seeds.

**Comments:** Extremely sensitive to high water tables that may cause trees to die after a few years of dependable performance. Under good cultural conditions, trees will grow to 30' in less than 10 years.

***Tulip poplar.*** *Both flower nectar and seed are utilized by birds.*

*Maclura pomifera* **OSAGE ORANGE**
**Family:** *Moraceae* Deciduous Tree
**Zone:** 5b
**Fruiting:** Autumn
**Size:** 50' × 40'

Native to Arkansas and Texas, this tree has become naturalized over much of the United States. It is often associated with poor, alkaline soils, but thrives in moist, fertile soils. Many legends are told about this tree, including the use of its wood by the Osage Indians for their bows and use in building construction. The knarled trunks support coarse, arching branches with tapering,

***Osage orange.*** *The seed, deeply imbedded in the core of this "horse apple," are the portion eaten by birds.*

lance-shaped leaves. Grapefruit-sized, warty fruit up to eight inches in diameter are green in summer, turning yellow-orange in autumn. Squirrels break open the tough fruiting body exposing the seeds, which are eaten by birds.

**Birds:** Purple finch, American goldfinch, and evening grosbeak.

*Magnolia grandiflora* — **SOUTHERN MAGNOLIA**
**Family:** *Magnoliaceae*
Evergreen Tree
**Zone:** 7b
**Size:** 100' × 50'
**Fruiting:** Autumn

The most widely grown flowering, native, broadleaf evergreen tree in the region. Magnolias are tolerant of a wide range of growing conditions, provided ample moisture is present. They will grow in full sunlight to partial shade, but sparse growth and flowering occur in shade. The large, white, fragrant, bowl-shaped flowers are seven to eight inches in diameter in late spring and summer and occasionally into autumn. Cones, which are four to six inches long, open in late summer and fall to release bright, shiny, red seeds hanging on filaments.

**Birds:** Red-eyed vireo, white-eyed vireo, red-headed woodpecker, gray catbird, Eastern kingbird, mockingbird, American robin, brown thrasher, wood thrush, red-bellied woodpecker, pileated woodpecker, starling, and cardinal.

**Comments:** This tree is extremely sensitive to being planted too deeply. Relatively high maintenance is associated with this magnolia because of leafdrop throughout the year. Trees may be eight or more years old before flowering. Several improved cultivars are available including: 'Majestic Beauty,' 'St. Mary,' and 'Samuel Sommers.' Birds have been observed feeding on other species of magnolias. The red pulp surrounding the seed is oily and high in lipids.

**Southern magnolia.** *Some birds eat the whole seed, while the red-eyed vireo eats only the red pulp.*

*Malus angustifolia* — **SOUTHERN CRAB APPLE**
**Family:** *Rosaceae*
Deciduous Tree
**Zone:** 6b
**Fruiting:** Autumn
**Size:** 20' × 15'

A small, native flowering tree is widely distributed, but loss of habitat has reduced the population. Normally associated with relatively heavy soils along woodland edges, this handsome tree will grow in full sunlight to partial shade. Dark rosy pink buds open into light, shell-pink, fragrant flowers in clusters of five in early spring. The hard, apple-shaped fruits, three-fourth inch or more in diameter are green, turning yellow-green as they mature in autumn. It is the only flowering crab that is really well adapted to the lower South.

***Southern crab apple.*** *Pink flowers followed by yellowish green fruit in fall.*

**Comments:** Relatively short-lived, usually under 15 years, it is susceptible to many diseases associated with the rose family. The edible fruits are used for jellies and canning.

*Malus floribunda* — **FLOWERING CRAB APPLE**
**Family:** *Rosaceae* — Deciduous Tree
**Zone:** 5a
**Fruiting:** Autumn
**Size:** 25' × 20'

Introduced from the Orient, this most popular of the crab apples has performed well over all of its hardiness zones in the United States, with the exception of the Deep South where it is short-lived. It grows best in a fertile, well-drained soil and full sunlight. The double, pink flowers appear in spring. Yellow or red fruits, depending on the cultivar, up to one inch in diameter mature in late summer and autumn.

***Flowering crab apple.*** *There are many species and cultivars, but 'Calloway' is a superior fruiting selection.*

**Comments:** Other species of the genus that are effective as small flowering trees and provide food for wildlife are: Siberian crab apple (*M. baccata*) produces white, fragrant flowers and red to yellow fruit; Sargent crab apple (*M. Sargentii*) has pure white fragrant flowers and small, dark red fruit; River's crab apple (*M. spectabilis* 'Riversii') has double pink blooms to two inches in diameter with green, non-showy fruit. There are many cultivars from these species.

**Birds that feed on crab apples:** American robin, red-headed and red-bellied woodpecker, tufted titmouse, mockingbird, gray catbird, Eastern bluebird, cedar waxwing, starling, evening grosbeak, purple finch, northern oriole, orchard oriole, blue jay, and rufous-sided towhee.

*Morus rubra* — **RED MULBERRY**
**Family:** *Moraceae* — Deciduous Tree
**Zone:** 6a
**Fruiting:** Spring
**Size:** 50' × 40'

This Oriental native introduced for use in the early Eastern silkworm industry has naturalized over the entire region. It thrives in fertile, acid or alkaline, relatively moist soils. Full sunlight promotes best growth. Mulberries tolerate considerable shade, but fruiting is somewhat sparse. Although fruiting for only about four weeks in late spring, it is among the most important fruiting plants for migratory and other bird food. This mulberry is distinguished from the paper mulberry by its more shiny, rough, veiny leaves that have marginal serration and are pubescent below. The multiple-seeded green fruits, similar to blackberries, first turn red and then black when mature. Trees may not produce fruit until they are six or more years old.

**Birds:** Red-bellied and red-headed woodpeckers; Eastern kingbird; great crested flycatcher; blue jay; tufted titmouse; mockingbird; gray catbird; brown thrasher; American robin; wood, Swainson's, and gray-cheeked thrushes; Eastern bluebird; veery; cedar waxwing; white-eyed and red-eyed vireos; bay-breasted warbler; orchard and northern orioles; scarlet and summer tanagers; cardinal; rose-breasted grosbeak; indigo bunting; purple finch; American goldfinch; rufous-sided towhee; and white-throated sparrow.

**Comments:** The number of mulberry trees seem to have decreased in the past forty to fifty years, as other trees have been selected for ornamental uses. Do not plant near paved surfaced areas due to staining caused by fruits and bird droppings.

**Red mulberry.** *Probably the best of all fruiting plants for bird food.*

*Myrica cerifera* — **SOUTHERN WAX MYRTLE**
**Family:** *Myrtaceae* — Evergreen Tree
**Zone:** 7a
**Fruiting:** Autumn
**Size:** 20' × 25'

A native, fast-growing, large shrub or small evergreen tree is widely distributed in the southeast and somewhat sparse in other parts of the region. Wax myrtle grows in thickets, woodlands, near swamps, in moist, acid soil, but tolerates a wide range of growing conditions. They thrive in full sunlight to partial shade. The aromatic leaves, to three inches long, are persistent. Grayish blue nutlets, up to one-eighth inch in diameter are covered with a waxy substance that has been in use since Colonial times for making scented candles.

**Birds:** Gray catbird, brown thrasher, Eastern bluebird, ruby-crowned kinglet, white-eyed vireo, yellow-rumped warbler, and rufous-sided towhee.

**Comments:** The most objectionable quality in well maintained landscapes is the heavy root suckering, but the dense growth provides an excellent bird habitat. It makes an excellent tree form, and screening as a clipped or unclipped hedge. Wax myrtle tolerates salt spray. The Northern bayberry (M. *pennsylvanica*) is very similar to the Southern wax myrtle, but is adapted to the northern part of the region.

**Southern wax myrtle.** *If you want to attract the ruby-crowned kinglet, plant this native.*

*Nyssa sylvatica* **BLACK GUM**
**Family:** *Nyssaceae* Deciduous Tree
**Zone:** 5a
**Fruiting:** Autumn
**Size:** 80' × 40'

A widely distributed native tree in the eastern half of the United States, this gum performs best in moist, fertile, slightly acid soils, but will grow well under less than ideal conditions. One of the last trees to leaf out in the spring and first to shed its handsome red leaves in early autumn. The dark purple, quarter-inch fruits are cherry-like as singles or in small clusters. They are about one-half inch in diameter. Fruits are quite showy in early autumn, after the foliage has dropped, and they provide an early source of wildlife food.

**Birds:** Eastern bluebird, gray catbird, Eastern kingbird, mockingbird, American robin, brown thrasher, summer tanager, starling, cedar waxwing, red-bellied and red-headed woodpeckers, gray-cheeked thrush, blue jay, tufted titmouse, rose-breasted grosbeak, and purple finch.

**Comments:** Berries are produced on female plants only. This tree is among the first to display its dependable, striking, purple color in very early autumn, but the early leafdrop is probably due to a fungal leaf spot.

***Black gum.*** *Blue-black fruit and red autumn color appear early and only female plants produce berries.*

*Ostrya virginiana* **AMERICAN HOP HORNBEAM**
**Family:** *Betulaceae* Deciduous Tree
**Zone:** 3b
**Fruiting:** Autumn
**Size:** 30' × 20'

A native, understory tree which is sparsely distributed on slopes and ridges in association with many other hardwoods growing near sandy streams. It grows best in slightly acid, sandy-loam soils, and in full sunlight to partial shade. Its growth rate is slow. The hop hornbeam has long, extended horizontal branches. Clusters of small nutlet fruits, which mature in autumn, are enclosed in a bladderlike covering.

**Birds:** Mockingbird, rose-breasted grosbeak, cardinal, purple finch, and American goldfinch.

**Comments:** Highly intolerant of disturbed soils and removal of overhead tree canopy, both of which may cause its death, but this tree has few pest problems.

***American hop hornbeam.*** *Seeds mature in fall and cling to tree, if not consumed by birds.*

## *Pines*

**Family:** *Pinaceae*

Naturally occurring and in reforested plantings, pines grow on millions of acres and comprise the predominant timber tree of the region. The wide distribution and some 90 species make up much of the natural woodland habitats. Pure stands of pines are not considered the preferred habitat of birds because most other species of plants are eliminated in carefully managed pine forests. Clear-cutting, a common practice in a silviculture system, results in a loss of biodiversity in plant and animal species, thus causing a reduction in the bird population.

Normally associated with upland, well-drained soils, pines will tolerate a fairly broad range of growing conditions, especially when used in home ground plantings where soils can be can be altered to provide acceptable growing conditions.

While a relatively large number of birds feed on the seeds, pines also provide a canopy of protection and cover for birds and shade-loving plants in a diverse plant ecosystem.

Birds eat the seeds which are exposed as the two-year-old cones open; the seeds are also collected and eaten on the ground where they fall.

*Pinus echinata* **SHORTLEAF PINE**
**Zone:** 6a
**Size:** 80' × 50'

This is the most abundant pine in the northern part of the region, thriving in sandy, well-drained soils. Needles are in bundles of two, sometimes three to five inches long.

*Pinus Elliottii* **SLASH PINE**
**Zone:** 7b
**Size:** 100' × 60'

This fast-growing pine is well adapted to the moist, well-drained soils of the southeast.

***Southern pines.*** *Most seeds fall from the opening cones and are eaten by ground-feeding birds. Row 1, longleaf; row 2, slash; row 3, loblolly; row 4 (top to bottom), shortleaf, Virginia, and spruce.*

Needles up to 12 inches long are produced in bundles of two's and three's.

*Pinus glabra* **SPRUCE PINE**
**Zone:** 8a
**Size:** 80' × 30'

A dense, low-branched pine for the first 15 to 20 years, it thrives in relatively moist soils along sandy streams and other lowlands. Twisted, wavy needles up to three inches long are in bundles of two's and have an olive-green color.

*Pinus palustris* **LONGLEAF PINE**
**Zone:** 6b
**Size:** 100' × 60'

This widely dispersed pine grows best in deep, sandy soils, but rate of growth is extremely slow for first three to five years and then rapid. The needles, to 15 inches long, are in bundles of three. It is the longest lived of the southern pines.

*Pinus Strobus* **WHITE PINE**
**Zone:** 2b
**Size:** 100' × 60'

Best adapted to the upper range of the region, this pine is characterized by its soft, bluish-green needle color. Needles that are five inches long are in bundles of five.

*Pinus Taeda* **LOBLOLLY PINE**
**Zone:** 6b
**Size:** 100' × 60'
An indigenous fast-growing pine of the coastal plains and the lower Piedmont Plateau, but will grow in most any well-drained soil. Needles to 10 to 12 inches long are in groups of three.

*Pinus virginiana* **VIRGINIA PINE**
**Zone:** 5b
**Size:** 30' × 20'

One of the best pines for poor, barren soils, the Virginia pine is extensively cultivated for Christmas tree production in the South. It produces stiff, twisted three-inch-long needles in bundles of two.

**Birds that feed on pines:** Carolina chickadee; brown thrasher; mourning dove; evening grosbeak; common grackle; dark-eyed junco; brown-headed, red-breasted and white-breasted nuthatches; pine siskin; chipping and white-throated sparrows; tufted titmouse; American goldfinch; American robin; Carolina wren; brown thrasher; cardinal; purple finch; house finch; rufous-sided towhee; blue jay; red-winged blackbird; and pileated and red-bellied woodpeckers.

**Comments:** Other pines which have ornamental uses and provide habitat and food for wildlife include the Japanese black pine, mugo pine, and Scotch pine.

*Prunus campanulata* **TAIWAN FLOWERING CHERRY**
**Family:** *Rosaceae* Deciduous Tree
**Zone:** 8b
**Fruiting:** Late spring
**Size:** 20' × 20'

This little-known late-winter- to early-spring-flowering tree is becoming more widely planted in the coastal South. It grows in well-drained garden soils in full sunlight to partial shade, but will tolerate heavier soils where drainage is good. The hot, rosy pink flowers are present some three weeks before most other spring flowering

***Taiwan flowering cherry.*** *Among the earliest spring-maturing fruits available to birds.*

plants are in bloom. It is the only known flowering cherry which produces an abundance of fruit in the lower South. The shiny, quarter-inch, red fruits turn black when fully ripe.

**Birds:** Mockingbird, cedar waxwing, and Eastern bluebird.

**Comments:** Easily propagated from seeds which germinate readily under fruiting trees, the small seedlings may be transplanted to a desirable location as soon as they germinate. There is considerable amount of genetic diversity within this species resulting in early to late flowering, which may occur before or after leaf development.

*Prunus caroliniana* **CHERRY LAUREL**
**Family:** *Rosaceae* Evergreen Tree
**Zone:** 7a
**Fruiting:** Fall and winter
**Size:** 30' × 15'

This widely distributed, native, small evergreen tree has been long used for screening and hedges. It grows in full sunlight to moderately heavy shade, provided soils are well drained. In natural woodland settings, it produces fruit sparingly. The dark, shiny, aromatic leaves, two to four inches long, appear along with racemes of white flowers in early spring. The large, black, shiny fruit to one-half inch in diameter, somewhat concealed by foliage, is prevalent during the winter and spring.

**Birds:** American robin, cedar waxwing, Eastern bluebird, and mockingbird.

**Comments:** Makes an excellent hedge plant in a pruned or naturally grown state. Highly sensitive to poorly drained soils, and is often killed by a root fungus. Poisonous to livestock.

*Prunus mexicana* **MEXICAN PLUM**
**Family:** *Rosaceae* Deciduous Tree
**Zone:** 6b
**Fruiting:** Autumn
**Size:** 15' × 20'

This little-known and not widely distributed native tree grows most often along woodland edges and as a weak understory tree in full sunlight to partial shade. It grows in most soils except those which are wet and poorly drained. Characterized by the dark, hard platelike, peeling bark scales and faintly pink flowers up to one inch. The blooms have a grape-juicelike fragrance. Dark

***Cherry laurel.*** *It is amazing that such small birds as waxwings can swallow such large berries.*

**Mexican plum.** *Late-fruiting and generally partially covered by a fungus, which detracts from its human eye appeal.*

purple, to nearly black, crab applelike fruit up to one and one-half inches in diameter ripen in autumn and persist for a long time.

**Birds:** Eastern bluebird, mockingbird, and red-headed woodpecker.

**Comments:** The largest of the native plums. It does not sucker like some others and, therefore, does not form colonies of trees.

*Prunus rivularis* **HOG PLUM**
**Family:** *Rosaceae* Deciduous Tree
**Zone:** 7a
**Fruiting:** Late spring
**Size:** 6'–8' × 8'

Useful as an understory tree which produces an abundance of white flowers in early spring, it is the best adapted plum for alkaline soils. The rosy-red fruits, to one and one-half inches in diameter, ripen in midsummer.

**Birds:** Eastern bluebird, mockingbird, and red-headed woodpecker.

**Comments:** A little-suckering plum and is probably the smallest of the native plums in its area of preference.

*Prunus serotina* **BLACK CHERRY**
**Family:** *Rosaceae* Deciduous Tree
**Zone:** 4a
**Fruiting:** Late spring
**Size:** 50' × 30'

Black cherry is a relatively short-lived native tree in the lower South; it thrives in most soils except swampy and very dry sites. It is widely distributed over the entire region and grows in full sunlight to partial shade, but fruiting is heaviest in full sun. Lustrous, peach-shaped leaves to three inches long have a coppery-yellow color in autumn. Small white flowers in drooping racemes

**Black or wild cherry.** *A very important fruit for migratory and other birds.*

**Hog plum.** *A prolific fruit bearer in a relatively small portion of the region.* (Photo by Benny J. Simpson)

appear with the leaves in early spring. Dark purple, to nearly black, somewhat showy fruits to one-fourth inch in diameter mature in early summer. The berries, steeped in alcohol or whiskey, make "cherry bounce"—a popular liqueur in Louisiana.

**Birds:** Pileated, red-bellied and red-headed woodpeckers; Eastern kingbird; great crested flycatcher; blue jay; mockingbird; gray catbird; northern and orchard orioles; wood, Swainson's, gray-cheeked, and hermit thrushes; brown thrasher; American robin; Eastern bluebird; veery; cedar waxwing; starling; red-eyed vireo; common grackle; scarlet and summer tanagers; cardinal; rose-breasted and evening grosbeaks; American goldfinch; rufous-sided towhee; and white-throated sparrow.

**Comments:** Fruits of black cherry have a high sugar content and it is one of the most important food sources for a large number of bird species in spring.

*Pyrus Calleryana* 'Bradford' **BRADFORD FLOWERING PEAR**

**Family:** *Rosaceae* Deciduous Tree
**Zone:** 5b
**Fruiting:** Autumn
**Size:** 35' × 25'

This is a selection of the Callery, a pear which was introduced from China as a root-stock for grafting most of the edible pears. The Bradford is noted for its dense, upright growth and heavy flowering. It was selected because of its tolerance to fireblight, a serious bacterial disease on members of the rose family. This pear grows in a wide range of soil conditions from dry to moderately wet and thrives in a well-drained garden soil.

***Bradford flowering pear.*** *Produces a profusion of flowers in spring and fruit and rich color in autumn.*

Clouds of white flowers appear with new foliage in early spring but last only a week to ten days. It is a very dependable, fast-growing tree for outstanding autumn color of red to purple. Clusters of russet-colored fruit, each up to one-half inch in diameter, are present in autumn and winter.

**Birds:** Gray catbird, mockingbird, blue jay, American robin, northern oriole, cedar waxwing, and purple finch.

**Comments:** Flowering and fruiting may not occur until the tree is several years old. There are many other selections available that may possess more desirable landscape characteristics. These include 'Aristocrat,' which has large, glossy leaves and is best adapted to the upper South. Where space is limited 'Redspire,' 'Capital,' and 'Chanticleer,' which have narrow, conical forms and ascending branches are other good choices.

## *Oaks*

**Family:** *Fagaceae*

Widely distributed over the entire region, and comprising a large number of native species, oaks are grown extensively for ornamental uses and are among our most important timber trees. Oaks are divided into two main groups—the white oaks that mature acorns in one season and have lobed leaves and without bristle tips and the red oaks which take two years to mature acorns and the leaves normally have bristle tips on the lobes. Adaptable to a wide range of soil conditions, oaks thrive in deep, rich, moist soils, although there are several which will grow under the stressful conditions of drought and poorer soils. Most oaks are deciduous, but the live oak, an evergreen, is probably the most popular tree in the lower South.

Comprising a great diversity in tree sizes, forms, leaf types and acorn sizes, there is an oak which will meet almost any situation where a medium to large tree is needed. Oaks, thought to be extremely slow-growing trees, will grow relatively fast during the first 10 to 15 years with proper watering and fertilization.

Acorns on all the native oaks mature in autumn and heavy production normally occurs in alternate years. They are an important source of food for birds, deer and other wildlife. While small birds cannot eat the large acorns, they can make use of these large nuts after they are cracked or broken open by animals and human activity such as foot and automobile traffic.

*Southern oaks (left to right): Southern red oak, Nuttall oak, Shumard oak, and cherrybark oak.*

*Quercus alba* **WHITE OAK**
**Zone:** 3b Deciduous Tree
**Size:** 60–100' × 50'

One of the more widely distributed oaks occurring from Texas east to Florida and north to Maine. Grows in bottomlands, rich uplands and on gravelly ridges. Performs best in full sunlight and a moist, fertile, well-drained, acid soil.

*Quercus falcata* **SOUTHERN RED OAK**
**Zone:** 6b Deciduous Tree
**Size:** 100' × 80'

This is one of largest of the red oaks. It grows in upland soils and has large, deeply lobed leaves that produce showy red autumn color. The acorns, up to one-half inch, are small for oaks.

*Acorns produced by oaks are eaten by many kinds of wildlife. Leaves and acorns of Southern oaks: (top row, left to right): white oak, blackjack oak, post oak; (bottom row, left to right): laurel oak, willow oak, pin oak, and Burr oak.*

*Quercus falcata* 'pagodifolia' **CHERRYBARK OAK**
**Zone:** 6b Deciduous Tree
**Size:** 100' × 80'

This oak is very similar to the Southern red oak, expect the leaf lobes are more nearly uniform and the gray-black bark somewhat resembles that of black cherry.

*Quercus laurifolia* **LAUREL OAK**
**Zone:** 8a Semi-Evergreen Tree
**Size:** 60' × 40'

This tree is similar to the willow oak, but differs in having larger, semi-evergreen leaves twice the size of the former. It prefers moist soils. This handsome tree is frequently used for shade and in street plantings. Leaves of the laurel oak are dark, glossy green and are twice the size of those of the willow oak.

*Quercus nigra* **WATER OAK**
**Zone:** 6b Deciduous Tree
**Size:** 100' × 80'

This red oak occurs in bottomlands but will tolerate as wide a range of soils as any oak. In the lower South, leaves may persist for most of the winter and twigs and branches continually fall from the tree making maintenance a year-round task. It is highly susceptible to mistletoe invasion. The relatively small, thin-shelled acorns are up to one-half inch in diameter and are easily eaten by birds. This tree is identified by the spatula-shaped, slightly lobed leaves. It has no significant autumn color.

*Quercus Nuttallii* **NUTTALL OAK**
**Zone:** 6b Deciduous Tree
**Size:** 80' × 40'

This oak has an oval to rounded canopy with relatively coarse textured leaves and upper branches are ascending, while lower branches are horizontal. Will grow in a wide range of soils from low, poorly drained clays to well drained ridges. Leaves are alternate, fine, to nine inches long, with the upper surface dull, dark green and the lower surface paler and glabrous.

*Quercus palustris* **PIN OAK**
**Zone:** 5a Deciduous Tree
**Size:** 80' × 60'

Best adapted to the mid-and upper South, this is among the most dependable red oaks for autumn

*Southern oaks (left to right): cow oak, live oak, willow oak, and water oak.*

color. It is a widely planted street tree in the eastern United States. It is also important for timber and firewood. Bright green leaves, to five inches long, have five to seven lobes. Acorns are up to three-fourth inch in diameter.

*Quercus phellos* **WILLOW OAK**
**Zone:** 6b Deciduous Tree
**Size:** 80' × 60'

Other than the long, two-to five-inch, willowlike leaves, this oak is similar in most respects to the water oak, but is a cleaner oak, not having the problems associated with water oaks: falling debris and extended leaf retention.

*Quercus Shumardii* **SHUMARD OAK**
**Zone:** 6b Deciduous Tree
**Size:** 80' × 60'

Considered by many to be the best of the oaks for shade and other ornamental uses, it is well adapted to the upper part of the region and has consistent red autumn color in the lower South. The symmetrically lobed leaves with tiny spines on the tips of the lobes are somewhat glossy. The acorns are three-fourth inch in diameter, making them edible by the large birds only.

*Quercus stellata* **POST OAK**
**Zone:** 6b Deciduous Tree
**Size:** 40' × 25'

A highly desirable native tree in size and form, but characterized by stout, gnarled branches with a heavy dense canopy of coarse-textured leaves. Usually absent from river flood plains and more commonly found on upland soils.

*Quercus virginiana* **LIVE OAK**
**Zone:** 8a Evergreen Tree
**Size:** 60' × 100'

This is the most popular oak in the Deep South. It is prized for its shiny, dark green, persistent foliage, which has considerable variability in size and shape. Live oaks should be reserved for large sites because of their broad spreading habit of growth. All leaves drop from the tree in late winter through early spring. Produced in great abundance in alternate years, the acorns are one-third inch in diameter.

**Other indigenous oaks of the region include:** escarpment live oak (*Q. fusiformis*), which is particularly well adapted to limestone soils in the western part of the region; overcup oak (*Q. lyrata*) is found growing in bottomland hardwood habitats in poorly drained areas; burr oak (*Q. macrocarpa*) has one of the largest acorns of the oaks and grows over the entire region and into Canada; cow or basket oak (*Q. Michauxii*), producing one of the largest acorns up to one and one-half inches in diameter, has outstanding autumn color; Texas red oak (*Q. texana*) another shrublike red oak which is normally under 15 feet in height and produces beautiful red autumn color; and Blackjack oak (*Q. marilanadica*) a "scrub oak" is a picturesque feature of the cut-over pineland where three or four trees growing together produce a symmetrical clump.

**Birds that feed on oaks:** Evening grosbeak, brown thrasher, mourning dove, red-bellied and red-headed woodpeckers, blue jay, tufted titmouse, white-breasted nuthatch, common grackle, rose-breasted grosbeak, and rufous-sided towhee.

*Rhamnus caroliniana* **CAROLINA BUCKTHORN**
Deciduous Tree
**Family:** *Rhamnaceae*
**Zone:** 6b
**Fruiting:** Autumn
**Size:** 20' × 15'

A large native shrub or small tree which grows well in full sunlight to partial shade. It thrives in a moist, fertile, acid soil and is commonly found growing on woodland edges. Large, veiny leaves up to six inches long are dark, shiny green and turn yellow in autumn. The one-fourth inch fruits are in clusters along the stem. They are green until late summer, turning red and then black in early autumn.

**Birds:** Gray catbird, brown thrasher, American robin, wood and hermit thrushes, cedar waxwing, and Baltimore oriole.

**Comments:** It has some of the most distinctive features in both foliage and fruiting characteristics of any of our native, deciduous plants, but is relatively short-lived and not well known.

***Carolina buckthorn.*** *The fruit color changes from green to red and finally black when ripened.*

*Rhus glabra* **SMOOTH SUMAC**
Deciduous Tree
**Family:** *Anacardiaceae*
**Zone:** 4b
**Fruiting:** Autumn
**Size:** 20' × 15'

A native, small tree that becomes quickly established and forms colonies in open fields, highway rights-of-way, utility corridors, and woodland ridges. Widely adapted to most soils, it thrives in full sunlight to partial shade. The compound leaves turn an outstanding autumn color in shades of red. This sumac produces compact clusters of crimson, fuzzy berries that persist through the winter.

***Smooth sumac.*** *The large clusters of fruit turn reddish before the other species complete flowering.*

**Birds:** Red-headed, red-bellied, and pileated woodpeckers; blue jay; Eastern bluebird; mockingbird; yellow-bellied sapsucker; ruby-crowned kinglet; northern flicker; red-eyed, white-eyed, and solitary vireos; gray catbird; brown thrasher; American robin; wood and hermit thrushes; yellow-rumped warbler; cardinal; and purple finch.

**Comments:** The most common of the sumacs for the lower South is the shining sumac (*R. copallina*), but apparently the berries are not eaten by birds. Other native species of the region that produce desirable bird food include: Fragrant sumac (*R. aromatica*), a three-leaf sumac resembling poison ivy, produces foliage that is aromatic and small red fruits that mature in spring. It thrives in limestone soils; Prairie flame-leaf sumac (*R. lanceolata*) grows to become a large, open sumac to 30 feet in height and has beautiful, scarlet foliage in autumn and red berries in winter.

*Sapium sebiferum* **CHINESE TALLOW TREE**
**Family:** *Euphorbiaceae* Deciduous Tree
**Zone:** 4b
**Fruiting:** Autumn
**Size:** 35' × 20'

A fast-growing native of the Orient, but widely distributed over the South, where it has escaped cultivation and naturalized. The population is so large that in some parts of the region, tallow trees have nearly become an uncontrollable pest. It is well adapted to most soils from moderately wet to dry in full sunlight to partial shade. The striking autumn color in reds, gold, yellow, and purple is a noteworthy feature. White, waxy seeds, usually three per pod, give the appearance of popcorn, and become quite prominent after leaves drop in fall.

**Birds:** Red-headed woodpecker, cardinal, blue jay, brown thrasher, yellow-rumped warbler, American robin, starling, mockingbird, and red-winged blackbird.

**Chinese tallow tree.** *The seed clusters of this tree resemble popcorn.*

**Sassafras.** *Few people see this fruit because it is eaten so quickly after turning this color.*

**Comments:** Somewhat short-lived, the shallow, competitive root system causes problems when trying to establish other plants near a large specimen. It is a messy tree because of the continuous shedding of plant parts.

*Sassafras albidum* **SASSAFRAS**
**Family:** *Lauraceae* Deciduous Tree
**Zone:** 4a
**Fruiting:** Autumn
**Size:** 60' × 40'

A native of the eastern United States, sassafras is widely distributed over the region, especially in open fields, fence rows, rights-of-way and woodland edges. The sassafras thrives on relatively poor, dry, sandy, upland soils in full sunlight. Leaves may be without lobes, two-lobed, and three-lobed. The autumn foliage turns brilliant yellow, orange, and red. Blue-black fruits, produced on female plants only, are up to one-third inch in diameter and ripen in early summer, but remain only a short time because they are quickly eaten by birds. It is reported that sassafras fruits about every three years. This may be due to freeze injury during flowering, since they flower in very early spring.

**European mountain ash.** *The most widely planted mountain ash in the northern part of the region.*

**Birds:** Eastern kingbird; great crested flycatcher; mockingbird; gray catbird; brown thrasher; American robin; hermit, Swainson's and gray-cheeked thrush; veery; Eastern bluebird; red-eyed and white-eyed vireos; and rufous-sided towhee.

**Comments:** The sassafras tree parts have medicinal, beverage, and culinary uses—oils extracted from the roots are used in beverages, while the dried, ground leaves (*filé*) are used to thicken soups and gumbos. A high lipid or fat content is present in the fruits.

*Sorbus americana*
**Family:** *Rosaceae*
**Zone:** 2a
**Fruiting:** Autumn
**Size:** 30'

**AMERICAN MOUNTAIN ASH**
Deciduous Tree

This native American tree produces clusters of bright red, one-quarter-inch fruits which are showy in autumn, although not as plentiful as the European species. The compound leaves with 11 to 17 narrow leaflets are greenish gray beneath. This species is more shrubby than treelike and is reported to be susceptible to borers, insect larvae that weaken and may eventually kill the tree. Provide a slightly alkaline, sandy, well-drained soil.

**Comments:** Although this is a native tree, it is recommended for plantings in the upper South only, and even here it is not a highly prized tree for ornamental uses.

*Sorbus Aucuparia*
**Family:** *Rosaceae*
**Zone:** 2a
**Fruiting:** Autumn
**Size:** 60' × 40'

**EUROPEAN MOUNTAIN ASH**
Deciduous Tree

This European import is by far the most popular and widely planted mountain ash in North America. It has been grown since colonial times and has naturalized in the colder regions of the country. It is adapted to only the upper South and does best in the higher elevations of the region. This mountain ash has conspicuous white flowers in spring and in fall the large clusters of bright red berries to one-quarter inch in diameter are very showy. Its combination of flowers, fruit, and autumn color make it an interesting specimen for most of the year.

**Comments:** Reported to be very susceptible to borers.

**Birds that feed on ashes:** Eastern bluebird, gray catbird, common grackle, American robin, northern oriole, brown thrasher, cedar waxwing, red-headed woodpecker, white-throated sparrow, veery, and wood thrush.

*Ulmus americana* **AMERICAN ELM**
**Family:** *Ulmaceae* Deciduous Tree
**Zone:** 3a
**Fruiting:** Late spring
**Size:** 100' × 80'

Once the most widely planted street trees in America, but due to Dutch elm disease, the population has greatly declined in the last few decades in the upper part of the region. Still, this stately, handsome, American native with thin trunks and broad arching canopy is frequently planted in the lower South where it seems to have escaped the disease. Elm performs well in fertile, moist soil in full sunlight, but will grow in less than ideal conditions. Greenish to reddish green, flattened fruits produced in dense clusters mature in late spring.

**Birds:** Red-bellied woodpecker, carolina chickadee, white-breasted nuthatch, American robin, red-eyed vireo, yellow-rumped warbler, house sparrow, northern oriole, cardinal, evening grosbeak, purple finch, pine siskin, and American goldfinch.

**Comments:** Two other outstanding native elms include: winged elm (*U. alata*), noted for its corky, winged branches, and cedar elm (*U. crassifolia*), a very clean tree that has relatively small leaves. These species are not susceptible to the Dutch elm disease and should be more widely planted as shade trees.

**American elm.** *Produces seeds in late winter or early spring.*

**Southern black haw.** *A large shrub or small tree which grows well beneath woodland canopies.* (Photo by Benny J. Simpson)

*Viburnum rufidulum* **SOUTHERN BLACK HAW**
**Family:** *Caprifoliaceae* Deciduous Tree
**Zone:** 6b
**Fruiting:** Autumn
**Size:** 25' × 15'

This is a native small tree with dark green, glossy foliage and produces pure white or creamy white flowers in late spring on spreading, somewhat stiffish branches. This viburnum grows well in moist soils and in full sunlight to partial shade. Clusters of dark blue fruit with a powdery-white sheen are present in moderate numbers in fall and are showy after the leaves drop in fall.

**Birds:** Eastern bluebird, cedar waxwing, cardinal, mockingbird, American robin, white-throated sparrow, hermit thrush, gray catbird, rose-breasted grosbeak, purple finch, red-eyed vireo, and white-eyed vireo.

# Shrubs

*Abelia × grandiflora* **GLOSSY ABELIA**
**Family:** *Caprifoliaceae* Semi-Evergreen Shrub
**Zone:** 5b
**Flowering:** Spring into fall
**Size:** 6' × 6'

This versatile, long-lived shrub grows in a wide range of well-drained, acid to slightly alkaline soils and requires full sunlight to partial shade. Outstanding characteristics include the glossy, bronze-colored foliage and terminal clusters of small, pinkish white, bell-shaped, fragrant flowers and persistent, copper-colored sepals throughout the summer into the winter. Many thin canes with relatively dense foliage provide an attractive habitat for birds.

**Birds:** Hummingbirds and good nesting site for many birds.

**Comments:** Relatively pest-free, abelia requires little maintenance other than an occasional removal of old, non-productive canes during late winter to keep abelia thrifty.

**Glossy abelia.** *A long-lived and persistent summer-flowering shrub.*

*Aesculus Pavia* **RED BUCKEYE**
**Family:** *Hippocastanaceae* Deciduous Shrub
**Zone:** 6b
**Flowering:** Early spring
**Size:** 20' × 10'; 8' × 6' average

Among the most widely distributed large shrubs or small trees of the region, the buckeye grows in a wide range of soils from moderately moist to very dry in full sunlight to partial shade. The palmately, compound leaves and the tall panicles of showy, red flowers are the distinguishing features of this native. The large, hard seeds, encased in a two-to three-inch pod, are poisonous.

**Red buckeye.** *Both white and red cultivars are available.*

When left undisturbed, volunteer plants will form groves of varying sized plants.

**Birds:** Hummingbirds

**Comments:** Since buckeyes flower very early, they are an important source of nectar for hummingbirds before most other plants are in flower.

*Aronia arbutifolia* **RED CHOKEBERRY**
**Family:** *Rosaecae* Deciduous Shrub
**Zone:** 3b
**Fruiting:** Autumn
**Size:** 8' × 5'

A native deciduous shrub which is often found growing in colonies with pines is adapted to most soils including those that are relatively dry and infertile. Found growing over most of the region, but not abundantly. Prominent, shiny red berries persist after the foliage drops. Fruit persists throughout the winter, if not eaten by birds.

**Birds:** Cedar waxwing, brown thrasher, Eastern bluebird, and American robin.

**Comments:** The cultivar 'Brilliantissima,' is worthy of much wider use in landscape plantings for attracting birds. However, it is not on published lists of food preferences for most birds.

**Red chokeberry.** *Large red berries on a not-well-known shrub.*

**Redleaf barberry.** *The barren branches of this popular barberry have bright red, shiny berries in early winter in the Botanical Garden at the University of North Carolina, Charlotte.*

*Berberis Thunbergii* 'Atropurpurea' **PURPLE LEAF JAPANESE BARBERRY**
**Family:** *Berberidaceae* Deciduous Shrub
**Zone:** 4b
**Fruiting:** Autumn and winter
**Size:** 3' × 2'

Best adapted to the upper South, the barberries grow in well-drained soils and will grow even in those relatively thin and infertile. Will not retain the reddish coloration of leaves in shade. The red fruit is a good winter food source for birds in parts of the region where it fruits well.

**Birds:** Rose-breasted grosbeak, American robin, Swainson's thrush, wood thrush, cedar waxwing, and ruby-throated hummingbird on nectar.

**Comments:** There are several cultivars of this species and some are very dwarf and have compact forms, but do fruit well. Other species of Barberry include *B. Julianae* and *B. Sargentiana*. There are nearly 500 species in this genus, but most are better adapted to the colder regions of the country. Remove old, straggly canes in winter to encourage a denser form and thriftier growing plants.

*Callicarpa americana* **FRENCH MULBERRY**
**Family:** *Verbenaceae*
**Zone:** 6b Deciduous Shrub
**Fruiting:** Late summer and autumn
**Size:** 6' × 6'

A highly popular native shrub with a mounding form that is tolerant of slightly acid to alkaline soil. It will grow in soils that are fertile to thin and is best adapted to woodland edges in full sunlight to partial shade. Leaf drop occurs well before the first frost, exposing long radiating stems with tightly clustered rose to purple colored fruit.

**Birds:** Mockingbird, cardinal, brown thrasher, wood thrush, American robin, rufous-sided towhee.

**French mulberry, or American beauty bush.** An *international plant also known as Spanish mulberry.*

**Bottlebrush.** *Hummingbirds battle over this species.*

**Comments:** The colorful fruit seldom persists all winter because it is so cherished by birds. French mulberry is among the early volunteer plants following land clearing, especially near woodlands. It is relatively short lived, but reseeds itself freely. The white cultivar, 'Lactea,' is less well known, but is becoming more available in the trade.

*Callistemon rigidus* **BOTTLEBRUSH**
**Family:** *Myrtaceae* Evergreen Shrub
**Zone:** 8b
**Flowering:** Spring and summer
**Size:** 8' × 6'

This relatively cold tender evergreen shrub grows best in well-drained soils and full sunlight. Expect periodic winter kills except in the lower coastal regions. In both Southern Florida and Texas bottlebrush can become a small tree. Bright, showy, red flowers are shaped in a bottlebrushlike mass. It withstands considerable drought and tolerates salt spray, which makes it a good seaside plant.

**Birds:** Hummingbirds.

**Comments:** Bottlebrush will not tolerate the heavy, poorly drained soils found in some parts of the region. Root rot fungus is a serious problem in heavy soils.

*Cotoneaster horizontalis* **ROCK COTONEASTER**
Semi-Evergreen Shrub
**Family:** *Rosaceae*
**Zone:** 5b
**Fruiting:** Late summer through winter
**Size:** 3' × 5'–6'

This low-growing, spreading shrub is best adapted to the upper South in areas with well-drained soils and full sunlight. Especially well adapted to raised plantings and rock gardens, cotoneaster is noted for its outstanding fruiting quality. It also possesses interesting branching patterns, pale pink spring flowers, and red autumn foliage if grown in the colder parts of the region.

**Comments:** While this is one of the best cotoneasters for the region, there are many other selections that will produce fruits varying in color from red to black that persist for long periods.

***Rock cotoneaster.*** *A shrub reliable for heavy fruiting in the upper South.*

*Cotoneaster lactea* **RED CLUSTER-BERRY COTONEASTER**
Evergreen Shrub
**Family:** *Rosaceae*
**Zone:** 5b
**Fruiting:** Autumn
**Size:** 12' × 10'

This evergreen cotoneaster is sometimes known as *C. Parneyi*. It is a broadly arching shrub with leaves one to three inches long and up to two inches wide. In spring, it has clusters of white flowers two to two and one-half inches in diameter. Red, quarter-inch fruits are present in large clusters in fall. Plant this cotoneaster in well-drained soil in full sunlight to partial shade.

**Comments:** Best adapted to the middle and upper South and is one of the best evergreen fruiting shrubs in this area.

**Birds that eat cotoneasters:** Eastern bluebird, cedar waxwing, American robin, purple finch, and wood thrush

***Red cluster-berry cotoneaster.*** *An evergreen shrub with clusters of red berries for the middle and upper South.* (Photo by William Fountain)

*Elaeagnus multiflora* **GUMI**
**Family:** *Elaeagnaceae* Evergreen Shrub
**Zone:** 5b
**Fruiting:** Late spring
**Size:** 8' × 6'–8'

This frequently overlooked large shrub will grow in full sunlight to partial shade in a wide range of soil types and with little care. The small, scarlet-colored, cherrylike solitary fruits are borne on slender stalks. When heavy fruiting occurs, the shrub is spectacular. In addition to being a favorite bird food, the fruit may be eaten fresh or used to prepare jelly, jam and marmalade.

**Birds:** Eastern bluebird, cardinal, gray catbird, yellow-breasted chat, blue jay, mockingbird, American robin, summer tanager, brown thrasher, and red-bellied woodpecker.

**Comments:** Not readily available in the trade, this dependable evergreen is worthy of much wider use in landscape developments because of its ease of growth and freedom from plant pests.

***Gumi.*** *Fruit is edible and can be used in jellies.*

*Elaeagnus pungens* **RUSSIAN OLIVE or ELAEAGNUS**
**Family:** *Elaeagnaceae* Evergreen Shrub
**Zone:** 6b
**Fruiting:** Late winter and spring
**Size:** 15' × 15'

A native of the Orient, the Russian olive grows best in a well-drained soil and full sunlight, but will tolerate considerable shade where it takes on a vinelike character. It is tolerant of limestone soils and coastal conditions, and well adapted to the stressful situations of urban areas. Elaeagnus grows rapidly, forming a dense, ground covering, impenetrable mass which provides excellent cover and nesting sites for birds. The flecked, silvery fruits up to one-half inch in diameter appear early in the year.

**Birds:** Eastern bluebird, mockingbird, and American robin.

**Comments:** Russian olive is highly drought tolerant with no major plant pests. Spines are present on the new, willowy growth shoots.

***Russian olive or elaeagnus.*** *Clipped hedge provides dense nesting sites and cover.*

*Erythrina herbaceae* **CORALBEAN or MAMOU**

**Family:** *Leguminosae* Perennial Shrub
**Zone:** 8a
**Flowering:** Late spring and summer
**Size:** 3'–5' × 3'

This native woody, shrublike perennial grows best in full sunlight to partial shade and tolerates a wide range of soil conditions. In most of the region, the top freezes back to the ground in winter. Clumps of fast-growing shoots return in early spring. These produce tall, leafless spikes of bright red, tubular, spurlike flowers in summer.

**Birds:** Hummingbirds.

**Comments:** Highly unpredictable growth habit, it is sometimes weedy and rangy with many suckers coming from a central crown; at other times, it is dense and more shrublike. Bright red beans are produced in pealike pods in autumn. Pest free.

**Coralbean or Mamou.** *Has showy flowers followed by capsules containing pealike, bright, scarlet seeds.*

*Euonymus alata* **WINGED EUONYMUS or BURNING BUSH**

**Family:** *Celastraceae* Deciduous Shrub
**Zone:** 3a
**Fruiting:** Autumn
**Size:** 8'–10' × 6'

This Asiatic native grows well in a wide range of soil types and even in shallow ones. It grows best in full sunlight, but will tolerate partial shade. It is an excellent shrub for the upper South, but preforms poorly in other parts of the region. Inconspicuous yellow flowers in spring are followed by purplish cap-shaped pods, which open in autumn to expose one to three orange-red seeds. Branches have two to four corky wings and these give this plant the common name, winged euonymus. The foliage turns a brilliant red in fall, making it one of the most desirable shrubs for autumn color. Winged euonymus is a very hardy plant and has a moderate rate of growth.

**Winged euonymus or burning bush.** *Excellent autumn color in the upper South.*

**Comments:** *Euonymus alata compacta* is equally as fine, but has lower and denser growth. It ordinarily grows four to five feet in height and makes an excellent hedge plant.

*Euonymus americana* **STRAWBERRY BUSH or WAHOO**
**Family:** *Celastraceae*
Deciduous Shrub
**Zone:** 5b
**Fruiting:** Autumn
**Size:** 6' × 3'

A native, understory species that is widely but sparsely distributed throughout the region. It grows best along streams, woodland edges and bluffs and prefers a moist, fertile, acid, well-drained soil with a high humus content. Performs well in shaded locations, but the growth rate is relatively slow. The most distinguishing characteristics are green stems and the capsulelike fruits which are about one inch in diameter and resemble a strawberry. The fruit capsules split open in fall to expose four to five orange seeds.

**Comments:** Under ideal conditions, a large specimen will give rise to colonies of thin, open canes formed from its underground stems. It is propagated by division of clumps and seeds.

***Fatsia.*** *Birds clean this plant of its fruit before many people see it in this ripened state.*

***Strawberry bush or wahoo.*** *Birds love this fruit and deer relish it, thus the common name "deer ice cream."*

**Birds that feed on Euonymus:** Eastern bluebird, mockingbird, wood thrush, fox sparrow, and yellow-rumped warbler.

*Fatsia japonica* **FATSIA**
**Family:** *Araliaceae*
Evergreen Shrub
**Zone:** 7b
**Fruiting:** Late winter to spring
**Size:** 6' × 4'

This relatively slow-growing, coarse-textured shrub introduced from Japan is widely used in the lower half of the region where soils are slightly acid and well-drained. It prefers partial shade, but will grow well in morning sun. The rounded clusters of berrylike fruits turn black when ripe. Late winter freezes often kill the flowers and developing fruit in the upper range of its adaptability. Other landscape values include its dark green, leathery foliage, and shade tolerance.

**Birds:** Mockingbird, cardinal, and blue jay.

**Comments:** Fruits are eaten by birds as soon as they turn black.

**Huckleberry.** *Provides birds food over an extended period in summer.*

*Gaylussacia dumosa* **HUCKLEBERRY**
**Family:** *Ericaceae* Semi-Evergreen Shrub
**Zone:** 5a
**Fruiting:** Late spring and summer
**Size:** 6' × 4'

A semi-evergreen native shrub which performs well as an understory plant in pine woodlands and on the edges of other forested areas. It prefers a sandy, acid, well-drained soil, but is tolerant of a relatively wide range of conditions. Flowering in late winter to early spring, the fruit matures quite early on this blueberry relative. The small, black fruits ripen unevenly and are never in great abundance at any one time. The long fruiting season provides bird food over an extended period of two months or more. Huckleberry is slow growing and one of relatively few native shrubs which maintains an intermediate height for many years.

**Birds:** Eastern bluebird, blue jay, mockingbird, cardinal, rufous-sided towhee, and gray catbird.

**Comments:** In most of its range, the huckleberry has beautiful red foliage until hard freezes, which may not occur until early January in the lower South. The fruit, high in sugar content, has been long favored for making pies and jams. Sometimes listed as *Vaccinium*, which also include the blueberries.

*Hibiscus rosa-sinensis* **CHINESE HIBISCUS**
Tropical Shrub
**Family:** *Malvaceae*
**Zone:** 10b
**Flowering:** Summer and autumn
**Size:** 6'–8' × 4'

A tropical, woody shrub native of Asia, that is planted as an annual in beds or in containers in most of the region. It is a year-round flowering perennial shrub in areas which are frost free. Provide full sunlight, and moist, fertile, well-drained soils. The large, showy flowers, up to six inches in diameter, appear throughout the growing season. Flower color ranges from yellow, orange, pink, red, white, variegated and bi-colors in singles and doubles.

**Birds:** Hummingbirds.

**Comments:** Profuse flowering is in late summer and autumn after the rate of plant growth is reduced. Low levels of nitrogen result in more flowering.

**Chinese hibiscus.** *Widely planted in the tropics and used as a container specimen in the colder parts of the region.*

*Evergreen hollies that grow in Southern gardens. Top row, left to right: Chinese, Dahoon, American, Foster. Bottom row, left to right: 'Burford,' 'Lord,' 'Savannah.'*

## *Hollies*

**Family:** *Aquifoliaceae*

Hollies, world-wide in distribution, are among our most prized native and introduced species. This group comprises one of our best adapted and versatile ornamentals for landscape plantings. Among the hollies there are both evergreen and deciduous trees and shrubs valued for their fruit and foliages. The diversity in plant form from low, spreading shrubs to erect tree forms can solve many landscape requirements. There is virtually no part of the region where an assortment of hollies cannot be found. Their adaptability over a wide range of growing conditions from hot to cold, moist to dry, sun to shade, acid to slightly alkaline or combinations of these are just a few of their many noteworthy qualities. Some hollies bear an abundance of fruit while others produce none—the reason being that most individual hollies have either male or female flowers, and berries are produced only on the female plant. Only when plants of both sexes are grown in close proximity are berries produced. A few of the Asian selections, like the Burford, will set fruit without pollination and fertilization. Some hollies may be pollinated by a different holly species.

Hollies provide the greatest source of bird food, cover and nesting sites of any plant material. Among the species, there are selections that set and mature fruit early in the season, while others set and mature fruits later—making food available for birds over a several month period. There seems to be that magic "time" when a particular holly fruit is desirable for bird consumption. Even though birds and berries are present together, the fruit is not eaten by the birds until certain changes have occurred, thus making the berries a food of choice. There seems to be an order of preference. It has been observed that the

American holly (*I. opaca*) berries are cleaned from the trees early in the season, while the possum haw (*I. decidua*), especially the orange-colored selection, and the Burford (*I. cornuta* 'Burfordii') are not eaten until later in the season, if at all. In years when there is an abundance of other available foods, some kinds of holly berries are not eaten by birds.

**Birds that eat holly berries:** Cedar waxwing, Eastern bluebird, mockingbird, American robin, brown thrasher, rufous-sided towhee, red-bellied woodpecker, hermit thrush, and blue jay.

*Ilex ambigua* **CAROLINA or MOUNTAIN HOLLY**
**Zone:** 7b
**Size:** 6'–8' × 5' Deciduous Shrub

In autumn, this little known native deciduous holly produces an abundance of translucent, round, red berries about one-fourth inch in diameter. A major feature of this species is its adaptability to poor, thin soils and cultural neglect. There are no known plant pests.

**Carolina holly.** *A holly which should be much more widely planted because of its ease of cultivation and outstanding fruiting qualities.*

*Ilex x attenuata* 'Fosteri' **FOSTER'S HOLLY**
**Zone:** 7a
**Size:** 20' × 12' Evergreen Large Shrub

This is a hybrid between two native species, the American and dahoon hollies. The most distinguishing characteristics are its slender, dark green, glossy leaves and an abundance of large, showy red fruit. It is an excellent species for decorative indoor use. Provide a moist, fertile, well-drained, slightly acid soil and full sunlight for best results.

*Ilex Cassine* **CASSINE or DAHOON HOLLY**
**Zone:** 7b
**Size:** 20' × 12' Evergreen Shrub

Highly adaptable to relatively heavy, poorly drained, slightly acid soils, this holly grows well in full sunlight to partial shade and has yellow-green foliage. Fruits are reddish-orange. This species is noted for its excellent screening and hedge uses and lending itself to clipping. A good variety is *I. Cassine* 'Myrtifolia' which is similar in all respects to the dahoon, but has very narrow leaves and larger red berries.

*Ilex cornuta* **CHINESE HOLLY**
**Zone:** 7b Evergreen Shrub
**Size:** 25' × 15'

Among the most widely cultivated of the Chinese group, this dense, mammoth-sized evergreen with spiny foliage produces large, scarlet-colored berries in great profusion. It grows best in full sunlight in a fertile, well-drained, slightly acid soil, but will tolerate a broad range of soil types, even heavy clay soils. Like all in the Chinese ('Cornuta') group, the tea-scale insect is sometimes a serious pest, as all hollies of the Chinese group are susceptible to it.

*Ilex cornuta* 'Burfordii' **BURFORD HOLLY**
**Zone:** 8a Evergreen Shrub
**Size:** 25' × 15'

The most widely planted of the Chinese group in the mid-to lower South, it grows well in a wide range of soil conditions from relatively wet to dry soils. Burfords produce huge amounts of scarlet-red fruits which persist late into the spring. The dwarf form of the Burford grows to about six to eight feet, but may not produce fruit in such abundance as the common Burford. Dwarf Burford leaves have a single spine, whereas *I. cornuta* have up to seven.

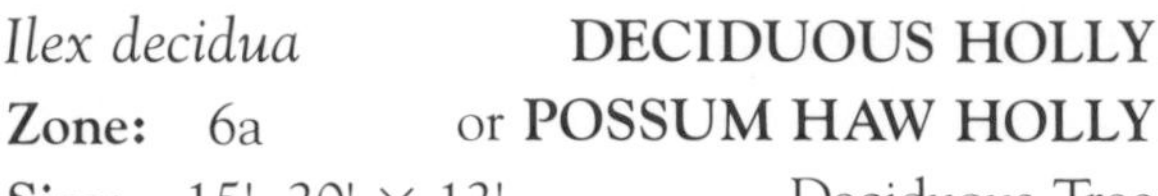

*Ilex decidua* **DECIDUOUS HOLLY**
**Zone:** 6a or **POSSUM HAW HOLLY**
**Size:** 15'–20' × 12' Deciduous Tree

A prevalent large shrub or small tree found growing in marginally wet soils along streams, swamp edges, and very prominent in fence rows where birds have dropped seeds. Before frost, the foliage drops to expose branches heavily laden with the yellow to orange to red fruits which persist until new growth begins in the spring, if not eaten by birds or other wildlife. In full sunlight, growth is more dense and fruiting is heavy. A variety of *decidua*, the Georgia Holly or longipes, is similar, but not as widely distributed, has more open growth characteristics, fewer fruits which are borne on extra long stems giving the fruit a cherrylike appearance.

*Ilex glabra* **INKBERRY**
**Zone:** 5b or **GALLBERRY**
**Size:** 8' × 5' Evergreen Shrub

This native, black-fruiting, evergreen holly is ordinarily found growing in wet to boggy soil of pinelands and prairies. It seldom grows over 5 feet in height, but will grow taller in cultivated plantings. In an undisturbed setting, large

*Georgia holly fruit.*

**Deciduous holly.** *The fruit of this tree is revealed after early leaf drop in autumn.*

colonies are produced by underground stems. Inkberry grows in full sunlight to partial shade and when cultivated it grows large and fruits moderately heavy. In autumn, the black fruit can be up to one-third inch in diameter. A white-fruiting selection is somewhat rare.

**Holly berries.** *Probably occur in greater abundance than fruit of any other shrub. Here an American robin is enjoying berries of an American holly selection on the campus of Clemson University.*

*Ilex opaca* **AMERICAN HOLLY**
**Zone:** 5a Evergreen Tree
**Size:** to 50' × 25'

This is the largest of all the native hollies. It is a highly prized tree that lives long and lends itself to a wide range of landscape uses from a single specimen tree to a thickly planted mass for screening. Characterized by its yellow-green foliage and large red fruit, this holly is well adapted to a wide range of growing conditions from marginally wet to dry, in fertile or poor soils. It will grow in full sunlight to partial shade. The upright conical form makes it a striking accent plant. There are numerous cultivars available in the trade including: 'Callaway,' with yellow fruit; 'Hume #2' with darker green foliage and a profusion of dark red berries; and many more. The most poplar hybrid is 'Savannah,' a pyramidal form tree with leaves having three to five spines and wavy edges.

**Inkberry or gallberry.** *Among the few black-fruiting hollies. Tolerant of salt spray, thus making it a good choice for coastal plantings.*

*Ilex verticillata* **WINTERBERRY**
**Zone:** 5a Deciduous Shrub
**Size:** 20' × 15'

Noted for its unusually large and striking fruit, this holly requires an acid soil and tolerates a relatively wide range of moisture conditions. Grown in full sunlight, the form is dense and it produces a large quantity of berries which may be up to one-half inch diameter. It is probably the most cold hardy of all the American hollies.

**Winterberry.** *A large, deciduous shrub or small tree which produces prominent berries in winter.*

**Yaupon.** *The most common native holly of the region; berries eaten by many birds.*

*Ilex vomitoria* **YAUPON**
**Zone:** 6b Evergreen Shrub
**Size:** 25' × 15'

The best adapted and most widely distributed native evergreen holly in the region, this species has many versatile landscape uses. It is often grown in multistemmed colonies, clipped hedges, or as a single, accent specimen in highly refined to naturalistic settings. It is reported to be more tolerant of alkaline soils than most hollies. The one-eighth inch, translucent, glasslike, red berries are produced in great abundance on female plants. A most prized holly for bird food, it provides an attractive habitat in both native stands and in cultivated situations. In native stands, male, non-fruit producing plants outnumber females by as much as eight to one. The weeping form, *Ilex vomitoria* 'Pendula,' is similar, except for its pendulous, down curving branches which hang closely to the main trunks. *Ilex vomitoria* 'Nana,' the dwarf yaupon, is normally a male plant and thus not produce fruit.

*Ixora coccinea* **FLAME-OF-THE-WOODS**
**Family:** *Rubiaceae* Evergreen Shrub
**Zone:** 9b
**Flowering:** Summer
**Size:** 4' to 6'

Ixora are hardy only in southernmost Florida, but can be used as summer bedding plants over the entire region. They are excellent container plants for the hot, sunny patio and require a minimum temperature of 55 degrees F. Therefore, they must be protected from freezing temperatures in most of the region. Performance is best in a well-drained, moderately fertile soil and full sunlight. This species has large, nearly flat clusters of bright red flowers. Other species of *Ixora* come in a wide range of colors which include white, yellow, orange, pink, and red.

**Birds:** Hummingbirds.

**Ixora, or flame-of-the-woods.** *The bright cross-shaped flowers and cross-arranged leaves help to identify this tropical shrub.*

**Comments:** *Ixora* is among the best of the tropical evergreens for container plantings. Prune in February to shape plants and to encourage fresh growth. Culture of this plant is very similar to that for hibiscus.

*Ligustrum japonicum* **WAX LEAF LIGUSTRUM**
Evergreen Shrub
**Family:** *Oleaceae*
**Zone:** 7b
**Fruiting:** Autumn
**Size:** 20' × 15'

Widely adapted to most soil conditions, this popular ligustrum grows best in fertile, well-drained soils and is very susceptible to root rot when grown in heavy, poorly drained soils. Probably the most versatile of the large evergreen shrubs, it is frequently grown as a clipped or unclipped hedge and may be trained as a multiple-trunked specimen. Green fruit, one-fourth inch in diameter, later turning bluish-black, are prominent in terminal clusters in autumn and winter.

**Comments:** This is a good border plant that provides transition from the lower growing species to the tree forms. It is an excellent, dense, evergreen which gives cover and nesting sites for birds.

*Ligustrum lucidum* **TREE LIGUSTRUM**
Evergreen Tree
**Family:** *Oleaceae*
**Zone:** 8b
**Fruiting:** Autumn
**Size:** 30' × 20'

This Oriental native grows throughout the region where it is tolerant to most growing conditions from moderately wet to dry soils in full sunlight to partial shade. A prolific reseeder, sometimes considered a weed tree, this normally

*Common fruiting ligustrums of the South. Left to right; wax leaf ligustrum, tree ligustrum, and Chinese privet.*

volunteer tree produces an abundance of dark blue to black grapelike clusters of one-fourth inch fruits in late autumn and winter. The widely dispersed seeds germinate readily in garden beds where they are usually unwanted.

**Comments:** This ligustrum is a very reliable fruit-producing tree which is common in urban areas, where other bird food sources may be scarce. Its shallow, extensive root system makes the growing of other plants beneath its canopy difficult.

*Ligustrum sinense* **CHINESE PRIVET**
Semi-Evergreen Shrub
**Family:** *Oleaceae*
**Zone:** 6a
**Fruiting:** Autumn to winter
**Size:** 15' × 20'

This privet, introduced from China, has escaped cultivation and has become one of the most common, early volunteer shrubs on cleared sites and woodland edges in the region. Privets are so common that in most situations they are a nuisance, but are among the best plants for bird cover and nesting sites. Privets grow well in most any soil condition from wet to dry, and is a nearly uncontrollable spreader in fertile soils. Black fruits, up to one-fourth inch in diameter are abundant and prominent in fall and winter.

**Comments:** Unclipped specimens form dense thickets, but can be contained as a clipped hedge, as they have been cultivated in gardens for several hundred years. Groves of the privet help to prevent soil erosion.

**Birds that feed on ligustrums/privets:** Mockingbird, cedar waxwing, Eastern bluebird, purple finch, starling, cardinal, American robin, gray cat-bird, white-eyed and red-eyed vireos, great crested flycatcher, white-throated and gray-cheeked sparrows, Swainson's and hermit thrushes.

*Lindera Benzoin* **SPICEBUSH**
**Family:** *Lauraceae* Deciduous Shrub
**Zone:** 4b
**Fruiting:** Autumn
**Size:** 10' × 12'

A little known, but very attractive, spreading native shrub having strong horizontal branches grows best in a moist, fertile, acid soil containing a high humus content. *Lindera* can be found growing on sites that are often too wet for other native berrying species. It will tolerate full sunlight to partial shade. On female plants only, large, red, shiny berries up to three-eights inch in diameter are borne beneath the foliage and are especially showy in autumn after leaf drop. These seeds are high in lipid or fat content.

**Birds:** Great crested flycatcher; Eastern kingbird; Swainson's wood, hermit, and gray-checked thrushes; veery; red-eyed and white-eyed vireos; and white-throated sparrow.

***Spicebush.*** *Yields a spice-scented aroma when twigs are crushed. Fruit ripens in late summer before many other berrying plants.*

**Comments:** The aromatic foliage, yellow autumn color and freedom from insects make this native worthy of much greater use in the landscape.

*Lonicera fragrantissima* **WINTER HONEYSUCKLE**
**Family:** *Caprifoliaceae* Semi-Evergreen Shrub
**Zone:** 5a
**Flowering:** Early spring
**Fruiting:** Late spring
**Size:** 8' × 8'

This Chinese native does well over the entire region. It thrives in a moist, fertile soil, but is tolerant of most growing conditions even when neglected. Full sunlight is required for best flowering, however, it will flower fairly well in partial shade. In early spring, pairs of creamy white flowers, five-eights of an inch in length, appear in clusters in leaf axils on short peduncles. The flowers are highly fragrant and have a lemon scent. Small red berries, that are somewhat translucent, ripen in late spring. Berrying is erratic in the lower south, but much more dependable in the mid-and upper South.

**Birds:** Hummingbirds, orchard orioles, and Northern oriole (nectar); Eastern bluebird, mockingbird, cedar waxwing, evening grosbeak, gray catbird, and hermit thrush.

**Comments:** This mounding shrub is a favorite for old gardens of the South and requires little maintenance other than an annual spring pruning after flowering and a light fertilization at pruning time. Can be used as a single specimen and in groupings.

*Mahonia Bealei* **LEATHERLEAF MAHONIA**
**Family:** *Berberidaceae* Evergreen Shrub
**Zone:** 6a
**Fruiting:** Spring
**Size:** 5' × 3'

This Chinese native is widely grown in the South for its distinctive leathery, hollylike, coarse-textured foliage. Yellow flowers in winter are followed by grapelike clusters of bluish-purple fruit in spring. It grows best in morning sun and afternoon shade. Provide loose, fertile, well-drained soils for best results.

**Birds:** Mockingbird, cedar waxwing, rufous-sided towhee, and American robin.

**Comments:** Requires three to five years to get a clump well established to form a major multiple-stemmed specimen. Old, well established clumps should be pruned in late winter. Cut back one-third of the oldest and tallest canes, to about two to four inches above the ground.

*Nandina domestica* **NANDINA**
**Family:** *Berberidaceae* Evergreen Shrub
**Zone:** 6a
**Fruiting:** Autumn and winter
**Size:** up to 8' × 3'

A highly popular, pest-free, evergreen shrub that grows over the entire region, nandina will tolerate most conditions found in the average garden. It does well in full sunlight and considerable shade. The compound leaves turn wine-red in winter. Fruit appears in prominent, striking, grapelike clusters with individual bright red berries being up to one-fourth inch in diameter in autumn and winter.

**Birds:** Mockingbird, cedar waxing, and American robin.

**Comments:** It has been observed that birds eat nandina berries only after most other food sources have been exhausted. Heavy flowering and fruiting take place only in open, sunny locations.

***Leatherleaf mahonia.*** *When fully ripened, this fruit is eaten quickly but by only a few birds.*

*Odontonema strictum* **FIRE SPIKE**
**Family:** *Acanthaceae* Herbaceous Shrub
**Zone:** 8b
**Flowering:** Autumn
**Size:** to 6'

A tropical evergreen herbaceous shrub, which is likely to be killed to the ground in the upper limits of its range. Grows in full sunlight or partial shade. Performs well in any good garden soil, but prefers moist, organic, slightly acid ones. Terminal spikes of one-inch, crimson flowers appear in late autumn. In its tropical habitat, it flowers over an extended period of time, but in the South, it flowers only under short days of autumn. Flowering usually starts in October and ends with a hard frost.

**Birds:** Hummingbirds.

**Comments:** Fire spike is an excellent source of nectar for migrating ruby-throated hummingbirds and for those hummingbirds that migrate into the region during fall and winter from more westerly areas and Mexico.

**Fire spike.** *This fall-flowering tropical is an excellent nectar source for migrating hummingbirds.*

**Chinese photinia.** *Photograph made in January in a Ft. Worth, Texas, subdivision entrance planting.*

*Photinia serrulata* **CHINESE PHOTINIA**
**Family:** *Rosaceae* Evergreen Shrub
**Zone:** 8a
**Fruiting:** Autumn
**Size:** 20' × 10'

This large, dense shrub or small evergreen tree is widely distributed over the region, usually seen growing as a single specimen or in mass plantings for screening. It does best in moist, well-drained soils in full sunlight and will not tolerate wet conditions. The shrub produces large, coarse, thick, leathery leaves to eight inches long and six inch clusters of white flowers in early spring. The flat-topped fruiting heads consist of scarlet to red berries in fall and winter.

**Birds:** American robin, cedar waxwing, and mockingbird.

**Comments:** This photinia is not as susceptible to leaf and root diseases as are the more common red tip and 'Fraseri' photinias. These two do not produce fruits that are readily eaten by birds.

*Podocarpus macrophyllus* **PODOCARPUS, JAPANESE YEW**
**Family:** *Podocarpaceae* Evergreen Shrub, Small Tree
**Zone:** 7b
**Fruiting:** Summer
**Size:** 20' × 10'

This Japanese native is a widely planted evergreen shrub or small tree in the lower South. Its most distinguished characteristic is the narrow, upright form which makes it a favorite for screening and use as a clipped hedge. Podocarpus performs well in full sunlight to partial shade and requires a loose, well-drained soil for best performance. Rate of growth is slow, but over a period of ten or more years it may reach a height of over 20 feet. There are male and female plants. On females, seeds are borne atop an accessory part known as the aril. It is the aril which ripens to a purplish-blue, one-half inch structure resembling a jellybean that attracts birds in summer.

**Birds:** Mockingbird, American robin, and house sparrow.

**Comments:** Although called a yew, this plant does not belong to the genus *Taxus*, which are the true yews. Not widely reported in the literature as a bird food, but birds clean the fruit from this plant.

**Podocarpus or Japanese yew.** *The part eaten by birds is the lower reddish to purple portion.*

*Pyracantha coccinea* **PYRACANTHA**
**Family:** *Rosaceae* Evergreen Shrub
**Zone:** 7a
**Fruiting:** Autumn and winter
**Size:** 12' × 10'

This introduced species from Europe and Asia thrives in full sunlight where the soil is fertile, well-drained, and slightly acid. It has an upright spreading form with horizontal branches and dark green, glossy leaves of medium density. Plants produce white flowers in clusters up to two inches across in spring. Applelike berries about one-fourth inch in diameter are bright orange-red in autumn, winter, through early spring.

**Birds:** Eastern bluebird, mockingbird, brown thrasher, cedar waxwing, cardinal, blue jay, American robin, hermit and wood thrushes, purple finch, pileated woodpecker, and gray catbird.

**Pyracantha.** *An espalier of 'Victory' pyracantha, which also produces fruits eaten by birds.*

**Comments:** In the upper part of the region, the cultivar *Pyracantha coccinea* 'Lanlandei,' an orange-fruiting selection, is used because it is more cold hardy. Pyracanthas are susceptible to fire blight, a bacterial disease which normally limits their life span.

*Rosa* sp. **GARDEN ROSES**
**Family:** *Rosaceae* Shrub
**Zone:** 2b
**Fruiting:** Summer and autumn
**Size:** Varies

The rose family comprises over 100 species in the form of shrubs, climbers and trailers. Widely distributed over the entire region, roses thrive in well-drained, fertile soils, but are adapted to a broad range of growing conditions. They should receive a minimum of six hours of sunlight per day. Most of the cultivated hybrids are not noted for their showy fruit (hips) production, but many of the old-fashioned roses produce fruits that contain seeds eaten by a large number of birds.

Roses that produce an abundance of fruits that are eaten by birds include: Cherokee rose (*R. laevigata*), a Chinese, high-climbing, evergreen rose, produces large, showy white flowers with yellow centers followed by orange, pear-shaped fruits in late summer and autumn. It has become widely naturalized and many think that it is a native rose. Multiflora rose (*R. multiflora*) is a popular, large growing rose used for hedges, and produces many clusters of white flowers in spring and pea-sized, red fruit in fall. This is the rose which has been extensively used as a root stock for many of the improved cultivars. Prairie rose (*R. setigera*) is a low-growing, deciduous, native trailer that produces pink blossoms in spring followed by red, one-half inch fruits in fall. Carolina rose (*R. carolina*) is a trailer, normally growing under six feet that produces rose-colored flowers up to two inches across and red fruits in autumn. Macartney rose (*R. bracteata*) is an evergreen climber to 20 feet and has white, fragrant, three-inch flowers in spring followed by orange, one-inch hips in autumn. This is a Chinese native that has become naturalized in the region.

**Rose.** *Small hips may be eaten whole or only seeds eaten from larger hips.*

**Birds:** Mockingbird; gray catbird; brown thrasher; American robin; wood and Swainson's thrushes; Eastern bluebird; cedar waxwing; cardinal; evening grosbeak; dark-eyed junco; American goldfinch; pileated woodpecker; and fox and song sparrows.

*Russelia equisetiformis* **FOUNTAIN PLANT**
**Family:** *Scropulariaceae* Evergreen Shrub
**Zone:** 9b
**Flowering:** Almost all year
**Size:** 4' × 4'

A free-flowering tender shrub with slender, rush-like, hanging branches, the coral plant is successfully grown outdoors in frost-free areas of the deep South and in parts of Florida, where it has

**Fountain plant.** *The form makes this plant ideal for raised planters.*

escaped cultivation. During most of the year, many bright red, tubular flowers, one-half inch in length make a dazzling display. The fountain plant will grow in sun to partial shade and requires a well-drained soil.

**Birds:** Hummingbirds

**Comments:** The fountain plant makes an excellent pot plant and is very suitable for hanging basket culture. Potted plants should be kept moist during spring and summer and run on the dry side for the rest of the year.

*Sambucus canadensis* **ELDERBERRY**
**Family:** *Caprifoliaceae* Deciduous Shrub or Small Tree
**Zone:** 4a
**Fruiting:** Summer through autumn
**Size:** 10'–15' × 10'

Is one of the most widely distributed and abundant semiwoody shrubs or small trees in the region on woodland edges, rights-of-way and unmanaged open spaces. Elderberry grows rapidly in soils that are wet to fairly dry and forms large clumps. It grows rapidly with an upright, irregular, broad spreading canopy. White flower heads ten or more inches across appear from early spring to frost. The flowers are highly prominent, particularly during summer. Large heads of purplish-black berries are present from summer to freezes.

**Birds:** Pileated, red-bellied and red-headed woodpeckers; Eastern kingbird; great crested flycatcher; blue jay; mockingbird; gray catbird; brown thrasher; cardinal; Eastern bluebird; American robin; gray-cheeked, wood, hermit, and Swainson's thrushes; veery; cedar waxwing; starling; yellow-breasted chat; common grackle; rose-breasted grosbeak; northern oriole; indigo bunting; American goldfinch; rufous-sided towhee; white-throated, chipping, and song sparrows; and mourning dove.

**Comments:** Elderberry fruits are edible and are used in making wine. Can quickly become a pest in the garden, if not controlled. It spreads by both underground stems and volunteer seedlings.

**Elderberry.** *One of the most widespread native fruiting plants in the region. A mockingbird is gathering food for her fledglings, who are waiting in a nearby shrub.*

***Tree huckleberry or sparkleberry.*** *Form (trunk), peeling bark, fruit, and autumn color are outstanding features.*

*Vaccinium arboreum* **TREE HUCKLEBERRY**
Semi-Evergreen Shrub
**Family:** *Ericaceae*
**Zone:** 6a
**Fruiting:** Autumn
**Size:** 10' × 6'

This relatively slow-growing, long-lived native large shrub or small tree is widely distributed over the entire region's pinelands, rocky woodlands, and along woodland edges. It prefers an acid, moist soil, but is tolerant of most soils, provided they are well-drained. This huckleberry does best in full sunlight to partial shade. The foliage color, ranging from red to deep wine, is beautiful in late autumn. Small, bell-shaped, white flowers are present in late spring. The three-eighth inch, black fruits which ripen in autumn are edible, but they are less tasty than other huckleberries.

**Birds:** Mockingbird, Eastern bluebird, and rufous-sided towhee.

**Comments:** An outstanding feature of this huckleberry is the twisted, sculptural trunks with reddish-cinnamon colored bark on old specimens.

*Vaccinium* sp. **BLUEBERRIES**
**Family:** *Ericaceae* Deciduous to Evergreen Shrub
**Zone:** to 3a
**Fruiting:** Spring to autumn
**Size:** to 15'

Hybridization of the blueberries has yielded selections which are adaptable to the entire region and produce an abundance of high quality, large delicious fruits. Formerly only the "Rabbiteye" blueberries were present in the lower South. Blueberries must have an acidic, well-drained soil high in organic matter for best production. They will grow in full sunlight to partial shade. The bluish-gray foliage turns a bright, orange-red color in autumn. Early bell-shaped, white flowers are followed by bluish to blue-black berries up to one-quarter inch diameter for the new hybrids. Fruits ripen over a period of several weeks in late spring and early summer.

**Birds:** Eastern bluebird; gray catbird; yellow-breasted chat; blue jay; orchard oriole; American robin; white-throated sparrow; starling; scarlet tanager; brown thrasher; cedar waxwing; veery; gray-cheeked, hermit, and wood thrushes; rufous-sided towhee; red-bellied and red-headed woodpeckers; mockingbird; great crested flycatcher; northern oriole; and cardinal.

***Blueberries.*** *Eaten by many birds, so bird netting is necessary if you do not want to share the harvest.*

*Viburnum dentatum* **ARROWWOOD**
**Family:** *Caprifoliaceae* Deciduous Shrub
**Zone:** 4a
**Fruiting:** Autumn
**Size:** 15' × 6'

A native large shrub that is widespread, but not prevalent, grows well in a moist, acid, sandy loam soil that has a high organic matter content and full sunlight to partial shade. They have oval to nearly rounded, heavily veined leaves and have excellent red autumn color. Flat, terminal clusters of creamy, white flowers appear in spring, followed by glossy, blue-black clusters of fruit in autumn.

*Viburnum Lentago* **NANNYBERRY**
**Family:** *Caprifoliaceae* Deciduous Shrub
**Zone:** 3a
**Fruiting:** Autumn
**Size:** 30' × 12'

This large shrub or small tree is native to most of the eastern United States. Its erect growth habit makes it ideal for naturalistic plantings in partial shade to full sunlight. Provide a moderately moist soil. White flowers are in flat clusters to five inches across in spring. In fall, showy blue-black fruits to one inch long are very prominent after leaf drop.

*Viburnum Opulus* **CRANBERRY BUSH**
**Family:** *Caprifoliaceae* Deciduous Shrub
**Zone:** 3b
**Fruiting:** Autumn
**Size:** 10–12'

This deciduous viburnum produces an outstanding display of clusters of white flowers in spring followed by red berries in early autumn. The 3-to 5-lobed, maplelike leaves to four inches long turn a bright yellow in autumn. It grows rapidly in a wide range of soils, but performs best in well-drained, moderately fertile soils in full sun to partial shade.

**Comments:** This species grows very large in a short period and may require periodic pruning to keep it in bounds, but the 'Compactum' cultivar only grows to a height of four to five feet and yet produces an abundance of fruit.

**Arrowwood.** *Outstanding fruiting and winter color.*

**Nannyberry viburnum.** *The fruits are very showy after leaves drop.*

**Cranberry bush.** *This red-fruited viburnum is best adapted to the middle and upper South.* (Photo by Greg Grant)

*Viburnum Wrightii* **LEATHERLEAF**
**Family:** *Caprifoliaceae* Deciduous Shrub
**Zone:** 6a
**Fruiting:** Autumn
**Size:** 10' × 5'

This attractive fruiting viburnum produces six-inch clusters of white flowers in spring and equally large clusters of quarter-inch, maroon-colored berries in fall. This Japanese native is not particular as to soil and does well in most any type as long as the drainage is good. It does best in sunny locations, but will perform satisfactorily in partial shade and is well adapted to most of the region.

**Comments:** The viburnums are easy to grow and quite versatile, having both evergreen and deciduous types. There are many selections that are not good fruit producers, but have large, showy clusters of flowers and make excellent cover for birds.

**Birds that feed on viburnums:** Eastern bluebird, cedar waxwing, cardinal, mockingbird, American robin, white-throated sparrow, hermit thrush, gray catbird, rose-breasted grosbeak, purple finch, red-eyed vireo, and white-eyed vireo.

***Leatherleaf viburnum.*** *At the John James Audubon Arboretum near Gloster, Mississippi, the fruits of this native shrub are ripe and ready for bird browsing in October.*

***Weigelia 'Pink Princess.'*** *An old favorite from Colonial times that has enjoyed a resurgence in popularity because of the many new selections.* (Photo by Michael H. Dodge)

*Weigelia florida* **WEIGELIA**
**Family:** *Caprifoliaceae* Deciduous Shrub
**Zone:** 5a
**Flowering:** Late spring
**Size:** 8' × 8'

Weigelias thrive in any good garden soil that is moderately moist. They prefer sunny planting sites and do not grow or flower as well in partial shade. The Asian natives are better adapted to the mid-and upper South where flowering is more profuse. In spring, pink to red, trumpet-shaped flowers appear in the axil of the leaves in groups of three to four.

**Birds:** Hummingbirds.

**Comments:** Weigelias are associated with old gardens and are often used in mass plantings and for screening. Annual pruning, after flowering, is needed to remove old, non-productive wood and keep plants thrifty and within a manageable size range.

# Perennials, Annuals and Vines

*Abutilon pictum* **FLOWERING MAPLE**
**Family:** *Malvaceae* Semitropical Perennial
**Zone:** 10b
**Flowering:** Summer to frost
**Size:** 10' to 12' × 5'

This fast growing, semitropical, gangly, multiple stemmed shrub with maple shaped leaves may attain small tree size when winters are mild; otherwise it is grown as a warm season perennial. It grows best in moist, well drained soils and prefers morning sun to partial shade. The most outstanding features are the prominent drooping, bell-shaped, veined flowers on slender stems. Flower color is orange with crimson veins. Smaller growing hybrids come in colors of white, pink, red, and orange.

**Birds:** Hummingbirds and orchard oriole.

**Comments:** This popular exotic flowering tropical makes an excellent tub specimen for outdoor areas that may be viewed from inside the home. The dwarf selections are popular for hanging baskets. Cuttings root easily in late winter and early spring.

**Flowering maples.** *An introduced species the hummingbirds learn to feed on by inserting their bills between the petals.*

**Coral vine.** *Attracts many bees and other insects in addition to hummingbirds.*

*Antigonon leptopus* **CORAL VINE**
**Family:** *Polygonaceae* Perennial Vine
**Zone:** 8b
**Flowering:** Midsummer to frost
**Size:** Vine to 40'

This fast-growing, old homestead site vine produces an abundance of rosy pink or white flowers. It can be used where quick summer shade is needed on porches, garden structures, and fences. Killed to the ground by the first frost, its relatively light foliage can be easily removed from structures to provide winter sun. Flowers are produced in great profusion in late summer and autumn.

**Birds:** Hummingbirds.

**Comments:** The coral vine blooms best in sunny locations with well-drained soils of relatively low fertility and where the roots of old plants are somewhat restricted.

**Cross vine.** *Usually discovered when the old flowers have fallen to the ground from vines climbing high in tops of trees.*

*Bignonia capreolata* **CROSS VINE**
**Family:** *Bignoniaceae* Deciduous Vine
**Zone:** 6a
**Flowering:** Spring
**Size:** Climbing vine to 50'

A high climbing woody native vine which clings by tendrils to almost any tree trunk, telephone pole, wall or other vertical structures. It grows fast and withstands adverse soil and moisture conditions from very dry to wet. The flowers are grouped in clusters in leaf axils. They are two-lipped, tubular, with flaring lobes. Flowers are red outside and yellow inside and blooming starts in very early spring. This plant can be identified by the cross which is clearly visible when the stem is cut transversely.

**Birds:** Hummingbirds.

**Comments:** A vine which forms a relatively light tracery of foliage on walls and other structures. Due to early flowering it is a good source of food for hummingbirds at a time when other food sources may be scarce.

*Campsis radicans* **TRUMPET VINE**
**Family:** *Bignoniaceae* Deciduous Vine
**Zone:** 3b
**Flowering:** Summer into autumn
**Size:** High climbing vine to 40'

Adapted to nearly every soil type, this native woody vine is a rampant grower and may require annual pruning to keep it under control. Normally, it is seen growing on unmanaged sites. The trumpet vine will grow in full sunlight to partial shade, but flowers best in sun. It has orange-scarlet, trumpet-shaped flowers to four inches long that are borne in clusters and has an extremely long flowering period from summer through autumn.

**Birds:** Hummingbirds.

**Comments:** Each flower produces a pod which contains many seeds and plants reseed themselves freely, sometimes becoming a pest in highly maintained settings. Cultivars 'Madam Galen,' 'Yellow Trumpet,' and 'Crimson Trumpet' are highly promoted in the trade for their more preferred flower colors and growth habit.

**Trumpet vine.** *This and the Japanese honeysuckle are the most prevalent wild-occurring plants which bloom profusely when hummingbirds are present in the South.* (Photo by Greg Grant)

***Bittersweet.*** *Often found as a fence-row volunteer in the northern part of the region.*

*Celastrus scandens* **BITTERSWEET**
**Family:** *Celastraceae* Deciduous Vine
**Zone:** 3a
**Fruiting:** Autumn
**Size:** Climbing vine to 25'

A most prized native vine for autumn and winter holiday decorations, the bright orange-red seeds persist for lengthy periods when vines are cut and brought indoors. Bittersweet thrives in most ordinary garden soils and prefers full sunlight to partial shade. This vine is often seen growing on fence rows and over the tops of small trees and large shrub masses. It becomes especially showy after the leaves drop and the pods open to expose the colorful seeds.

**Birds:** Eastern bluebird, cardinal, mockingbird, American robin, and cedar waxwing.

**Comments:** This vine is best suited for the colder parts of the region. It is seldom seen near the coast.

*Clerodendrum paniculatum* **PAGODA FLOWER**
Tropical Shrub
**Family:** *Verbenaceae*
**Zone:** 10b
**Flowering:** Spring into fall
**Size:** 4'–6'

This tropical Asian shrub grows well in moist, loose, fertile, well-drained soils. Like most *Clerodendrums*, it responds well to relatively high levels of fertilization and performs best in full sunlight. The scarlet, tubular flowers are one-half inch long and are present most of the year when plants are grown under tropical temperatures. It may be used as a container specimen, but must be protected from freezes and does not grow and flower well when temperatures are cool.

**Comments:** The large, five-inch, lobed leaves and profusion of flowers make this plant an outstanding container specimen.

***Pagoda flower.*** *Produces blooms over a long period.*

*Clerodendrum speciossissimum* **JAVA PLANT**
Tropical Perennial
**Family:** *Verbenaceae*
**Zone:** 8b
**Flowering:** Late spring through autumn
**Size:** to 12' × 4'–5'

A semiwoody, upright, spreading perennial which is popular in old, Deep-South gardens. It is especially useful in center-city locations where it receives adequate protection from winter freezes. Even at its northernmost limits, plants return from the root system even after relatively hard freezes. Provide full sunlight and a moist, loose, fertile, well-drained soil: this large growing perennial will grow satisfactorily under conditions less than ideal. Spectacular, scarlet flowers appear in large panicles up to 18 inches above the coarse-textured, heart-shaped leaves from early summer to frost.

**Comments:** Relatively free of insect and disease pests. It normally suckers freely, forming colonies of varying sized plants.

***Java plant.*** *Looks like a Fourth of July fireworks display when it comes into flower at about this time of year.*

**Comments:** Produces flowers for an extended period when hummingbirds are present in the region.

*Clerodendrum splendens* **GLORY-BOWER**
**Family:** *Verbenaceae* Tropical Vining Shrub
**Zone:** 9b
**Flowering:** Late spring through autumn
**Size:** 4' to 6'

This tender tropical is suitable for outdoor culture only in South Florida and may be grown in other areas as a container plant that is given protection in a greenhouse during winter. The twining shrub has six-inch oblong leaves and many flowers are produced in six-inch cymes. It flowers almost constantly under tropical conditions, but only in the warm months when grown as a container specimen with minimum protection. It prefers a moist, well-drained, fertile soil and does best when grown in sunlight.

*Clerodendrum Thomsoniae* **BLEEDING-HEART**
Tropical Vine
**Family:** *Verbenaceae*
**Zone:** 9b
**Flowering:** Late spring through autumn
**Size:** Vine to 10'–12' or more

This tropical clambering vine from West Africa is suited for outdoor culture only in the extreme southern parts of the region. It makes an excellent outdoor warm season flowering plant for sunny locations, but must be given protection during winter. Provide it with a fertile, well-drained soil. Large clusters of white flowers with red, protruding centers make it an attractive container grown specimen. Provide a small structure, such as a lattice or wire frame, for support.

**Comments:** The cultivar 'Velectum' produces large clusters of rosy-magenta flowers, which provide color for an extended period.

**Birds that feed on clerodendrums:** Hummingbirds.

*Cocculus carolinus* **CAROLINA SNAILSEED**
**Family:** *Menispermaceae*
**Zone:** 7a Deciduous Vine
**Fruiting:** Late summer and autumn
**Size:** Vine to 30'

A native, high-climbing vine with relatively sparse foliage, this fast-growing vine prefers full sun and is well adapted to a wide range of soil types, from dry to moist. It must have some type of support and is often found growing on tops of shrub masses and small trees. In autumn the bright red fruit is produced in dense clusters that are two to six inches long and are easily identified by removing the pulp from the seeds to reveal the snail-shaped seed.

**Birds:** Eastern bluebird, mockingbird, and American robin.

**Cigar flower.** *One of the many* Cupheas *which are enjoyed by hummingbirds.* (Photo by Steve Hope)

**Carolina snailseed.** *Size ranges from a small, tame vine to a heavy clambering mass which may engulf the shrub forms over which it grows.*

**Comments:** This vine requires several years of growth before it produces fruit. It is a relatively non-invasive vine, often overlooked in its native habitat, that has many possibilities for landscape uses.

*Cuphea ignea* **CIGAR FLOWER**
**Family:** *Lythraceae* Perennial
**Zone:** 10a
**Flowering:** Late spring through autumn
**Size:** 3'

A tender perennial, normally grown as an annual or as a seasonal color container plant that requires winter protection in most of the region. In the extreme deep South, it is planted as a perennial in well-drained beds receiving full sunlight. The relatively small, one-inch flowers are bright red and tubular.

***Carolina yellow jessamine.*** *Early color and fragrance make this state flower of South Carolina a highly desirable vine.*

**Birds:** Hummingbirds.

**Comments:** The Mexican cigar plant, *C. micropetala,* has flowers that are yellow to orange, tipped with red, growing on tall, upright stems, three to four feet in height. This species requires the same growing conditions as the cigar flower.

*Gelsemium sempervirens* **CAROLINA YELLOW JESSAMINE**
**Family:** *Loganiaceae* Evergreen Vine
**Zone:** 7a
**Flowering:** Late winter and spring
**Size:** Vine to 40'

This very early spring flowering native vine dominates many of the woodland edges, growing to the tops of trees, over fences and hedgerows throughout the region. It is a dense, twining vine that thrives in full sunlight to partial shade in most any soils. As a cultivated vine, it is a rampant grower and must be pruned periodically to keep it in bounds. The bright, yellow, funnel-shaped, fragrant flowers appear in profusion.

**Birds:** Hummingbirds.

**Comments:** This dense-growing vine provides excellent cover and nesting sites for birds. It must be pruned every two to three years to remove old, non-productive stems to maintain its flowering vigor.

*Hamelia patens* **FIREBUSH**
**Family:** *Rubiaceae* Perennial
**Zone:** 8a
**Flowering:** Late spring into autumn
**Size:** 5'–6' × 5'

This fast-growing plant will generally survive outdoors only in coastal South Texas and south Florida, but will frequently return from the roots in areas further north. In most locations it must be treated as an annual bedding plant or used in containers for seasonal color. Provide the same growing conditions as for other tropicals such as Chinese hibiscus. It thrives in hot, sunny, dry areas, but responds well to good soil management, watering, and fertilization practices. Firebush does not grow well until the weather is hot, when flowering begins. Flowering is greatly reduced with the first cool days of autumn. The scarlet to orange-colored, tubular flowers are three-quarters of an inch long and are borne in clusters. Small, blue-black fruits, about one-eight inch in diameter are produced during the season. However, these are not very showy.

**Birds:** Hummingbirds feed on nectar and Northern cardinal eat the fruit.

**Comments:** Among the best flowers for attracting hummingbirds and worthy of much more use as a warm season bedding plant. Makes an outstanding container plant for the sunny patio.

Firebush. Does well in areas receiving little frost such as this one in Laredo, Texas. (Photo by Greg Grant)

**Firebush.** *Flowers are a hummingbird's delight.*

*Hedychium coronarium* **BUTTERFLY GINGER**
Tropical Perennial
**Family:** *Zingiberaceae*
**Zone:** 8b
**Flowering:** Spring and summer
**Size:** to 6'

This is the most hardy of the tropical gingers and can be grown farther north than other species; however, its range is still restricted to the lower South. It requires considerable amounts of water and can be grown in moderately wet soils and is tolerant to salt spray. In moist, fertile soils and partial shade, rate of growth is fast. It produces clusters of fragrant, white flowers on tall spikes above the foliage. This ginger is in continuous bloom for most of the spring, summer, and into early fall. It is generally killed to the ground with light freezes and periodic cleaning is necessary to clear away old, nonproductive growth. At the northern part of the growing range, it should be mulched with three to four inches of pine straw, leaves or other organic material to protect the over-wintering root system against extremely low temperatures.

**Comments:** Gingers form dense clumps and they may be divided every three to five years. Several other species of ginger may also be grown in extreme southern parts of the region.

**Butterfly ginger.** *Fragrance is as welcome as the nectar for hummingbirds.*

These include *H. Wilsonii, H. Gardeneranum, H. kewense, H. flavum, Alpinia Zerumbet,* and others which require the same type of soils and light conditions as the butterfly ginger.

*Helianthus angustifolia* **SWAMP SUNFLOWER, NARROW-LEAVED SUNFLOWER**
**Family:** *Compositae*
**Flowering:** Autumn
**Size:** 4' to 6'
Annual

This native sunflower grows solitary or in dense clumps and is widely distributed over the lower South, but generally absent from the alluvial flood plains. It will tolerate poor, droughty, soils and produce masses of two-to three-inch yellow flowers for a period of four to six weeks in autumn. This sunflower has long, narrow leaves that are only one-quarter inch wide and four inches long. The surface of the leaves is rough and hairy and the margins are enrolled. It often blankets open fields and roadsides, and is an excellent choice for naturalistic settings.

**Sunflower.** *Most popular seed for feeding stations.*

**Narrow-leaved sunflower.** *Makes a spectacular display of color in fall.* (Photo by Felder Rushing)

**Comments:** This sunflower is worthy of more use as a cultivated garden perennial. It will reseed itself and plants should not be cut back until the seed are mature.

*Helianthus annuus* **SUNFLOWER**
**Family:** *Compositae*
**Flowering:** Summer
**Size:** to 10'
Annual

This annual can be grown throughout the United States. Full sunlight and well-drained soils are essential and it is relatively easy to grow in the flower and vegetable garden. Mammoth-sized flower heads up to 12 or more inches across are borne atop stiff, erect stems. One flower head may produce hundreds of seeds which are eaten by wildlife and humans.

**Comments:** This sunflower, with a coarse-textured foliage, will grow in most garden situations and is among the showiest, fastest growing annuals. The seeds coats may be striped or black, but most birds prefer black seeds. Gather the flower heads with intact seeds after they become partially dry. Heads may be attached to feeding stations or trees in close proximity to bird viewing areas, or seeds may be removed from the heads and stored for later feeding.

*Helianthus Maximiliani* **MAXIMILIAN SUNFLOWER**
**Family:** *Compositae*
**Flowering:** Late summer and autumn
**Size:** to 5' or more

This annual is widely distributed over much of Texas, but will grow in sunny, well-drained soils in all other dry parts of the region. While the individual yellow flower heads are somewhat small, only about three inches in diameter, there is a great profusion of flowers on each stem.

**Comments:** It is a short-day plant that does not flower where it receives light at night such as from a street or safety light. Is excellent for wildflower meadows and will form colonies after becoming well established.

**Birds that feed on sunflowers:** Cardinal, Carolina chickadee, American goldfinch, house finch, purple finch, common grackle, evening grosbeak, blue jay, nuthatches, white-throated sparrow, tufted titmouse, rufous-sided towhee, house sparrow, dark-eyed junco, mourning dove, pine siskin, red-winged blackbird, scrub jay, and red-bellied and red-headed woodpeckers.

**Maxmilian sunflower.** *This western sunflower is prevalent in the open countryside.* (Photo by Benny J. Simpson)

*Ipomea coccinea* **RED MORNING GLORY**
**Family:** *Convolvulaceae*
**Flowering:** Summer
**Size:** Vine to 10'
Annual Vine

A fast-growing, summer-flowering vine that thrives in full sunlight in a wide range of soils, but performs best in a fertile, well-drained, slightly acid soil. The somewhat delicate vine can be used on trellis, lattice, and similar landscape structures to provide quick shade. The one and one-half inch, scarlet flowers are present all summer, but usually not in great profusion. It dies with the arrival of cold weather.

**Birds:** Hummingbirds

***Red morning glory.*** *Favored by hummingbirds but invasive of croplands.*

**Comments:** There are many morning glory selections which grow in the region, but this one is not as invasive as other members of the genus, making it a more satisfactory selection for most uses.

*Ipomea Quamoclit* **CYPRESS VINE**
**Family:** *Convolvulaceae* Annual
**Flowering:** Summer and early Autumn
**Size:** Vine to 20'

This delicate, fine-textured vine has become naturalized in the southern states. It performs satisfactorily in poor soil, but thrives in fertile, well-drained soil and full sunlight. Flowering is best when there is some moisture and nutrition stress. After being killed by frost, the vine is easily cleaned from garden structures on which it had grown. Numerous small, scarlet, trumpet-shaped flowers to one and one-half inches long are present from early summer to frost.

**Birds:** Hummingbirds.

**Comments:** This annual vine reseeds itself freely, giving it the appearance of a reoccurring perennial.

*Iris fulva* **RED LOUISIANA IRIS**
**Family:** *Iridaceae* Perennial
**Zone:** 6a
**Flowering:** Spring
**Size:** 4' × 2'

This iris is one of four native Louisiana species which have been grown for decades under ordinary garden culture with excellent results. Provide as much sunlight as possible, and never less than one-half day. They grow in wet, boggy conditions, but do equally well in a prepared garden bed. Foliage normally becomes unattractive in midsummer and remains so until new growth begins in spring. Copper-colored flowers appear in early spring and are an early food source for hummingbirds.

**Birds:** Hummingbirds and orchard orioles.

**Comments:** Many believe that hummingbirds feed on all irises, of which there are many. Closer observations reveal, except for this species, that the hummingbirds are only investigating the flowers as a possible food source and not feeding on them. Orchard orioles often shred the petals of this and many other irises to get to the source of nectar at base of the flowers. An excellent reference on the history and culture of Louisiana

***Cypress vine.*** *Makes a quick cover. Normally grown as an annual, returning each year from seeds.*

*Ruby-throated hummingbird feeding on Louisiana iris.* (Photo by Steve Hope)

iris has been written by M. Caillet and J. K. Mertzweiller. Check bibliography for additional information on this book.

*Justicia Brandegeana* **SHRIMP PLANT**
**Family:** *Acanthaceae* Perennial
**Zone:** 8b
**Flowering:** Spring through autumn
**Size:** 3' × 3'

Shrimp plant performs best in moist, fertile, well-drained soils where it receives a minimum of one-half day, preferably morning, sunlight. In the upper region of the zone it will be killed to the ground, but usually returns from the roots. Where it does not freeze, plants become straggly and unsightly and should be cut back in late winter. White, tubular flowers extend beyond the showy, salmon-colored bracts from spring until frost. Heavy flowering occurs in several cycles from spring until frost.

**Comments:** Common in old homestead gardens where they are afforded winter protection, plants form large masses and live for many years.

*Justicia carnea* **BRAZILIAN-PLUME**
**Family:** *Acanthaceae* Tropical Perennial
**Zone:** 8b
**Flowering:** Spring through autumn
**Size:** 6' × 4'

This perennial is hardy only in the lower South and will be killed where freezes occur. Widely used as a summer bedding or container plant over much of the region because of its showy pink flowers during the hot summer months. For best performance provide a moist, well-drained soil. It does surprisingly well in shade, although it prefers partial, morning sunlight. The plant has large, heavily veined leaves with two-inch,

**Brazilian plume.** *The warm pink color adds zest to the shade garden and attracts hummingbirds.*

**Shrimp plant.** *The showy part of this hummingbird plant is a rusty colored bract (modified leaf) resembling shrimp. Blooms the year round in tropical landscapes.*

funnel-shaped flowers produced in short, dense, pineapple-shaped terminal clusters.

**Comments:** This plant is often offered in the trade under the common name Jacobinia. Related species come in yellow and red.

**Birds that feed on Justicia:** Hummingbirds.

*Kniphofia Uvaria* **RED-HOT-POKER**
**Family:** *Liliaceae* Perennial
**Zone:** 8b
**Flowering:** Late summer
**Size:** 4' × 2'

This grasslike perennial is best adapted for hot, sunny sites with well-drained soils. The tops of the pokerlike, stiff stems bear many tubular-shaped florets in colors of yellow, apricot, orange, orange-red, and bi-colors in summer and fall.

**Birds:** Hummingbirds.

**Comments:** In the upper range provide heavy mulching to protect the roots in winter.

**Red-hot poker.** *A background planting adds vertical contrast to the low-growing hostas in the planting composition.*

**'Dallas Red' lantana.** *This cultivar is ideal for planters and other containers for small, sunny gardens.*

*Lantana Camara* **LANTANA**
**Family:** *Verbenaceae* Perennial
**Zone:** 8b
**Flowering:** Summer to frost
**Size:** 5' × 6'

This old-fashioned perennial has naturalized in the coastal south from Florida to Texas. It performs best in sunny locations with a well-drained soil, but grows in very stressful conditions. Lantanas bloom over a long period and survive along coastal areas where salt conditions prevent many other plants from growing. Flowering from late spring until the arrival of cool weather, they come in bi-colors of yellow, pink, red, and orange. Clusters of bluish-black fruits are produced by some varieties.

**Birds:** Hummingbirds feed on nectar and Northern cardinals eat the seed.

**Comments:** Some of the most dependable selections include: 'Irene' (magenta and yellow), 'Dallas Red' (red) and 'Christine' (pink). The recent introductions are generally under two feet in height and are heavier flowering, but do not seem to be as attractive to hummingbirds. Some of the popular selections in this group include: 'New Gold,' 'Lemon Drop,' and 'Silver Mound.' A few cultivars are sterile and produce no fruit, which is an advantage in that more flowers are produced.

*Lobelia Cardinalis* **CARDINAL FLOWER**
**Family:** *Lobeliaceae* Perennial
**Zone:** 3a
**Flowering:** Late summer and autumn
**Size:** 3' × 2'

This beautiful, red flowering, native perennial prefers moist, fertile acid to slightly alkaline soils in partial shade. The showy, bright red, tubular flowers up to four inches long occur on multiple-flowering spikes. They begin flowering in August when the hummingbirds start their fall migration, thus providing an important late season food source in naturalistic landscapes.

**Birds:** Hummingbirds.

**Comments:** Cardinal flower is one of the most admired wildflowers of the South, but many native stands are decreasing. Due to increased demands by the gardening public, commercial growers are producing this species in significant quantities. 'Queen Victoria' and 'St. Elmo's Fire' (hybrids of *L. cardinalis fulgens*) are recent introductions showing considerable promise.

***Cardinal flower.*** *Late-blooming, it is an excellent source of nectar for migrating hummingbirds. Widely distributed, but seldom abundant.*

***Japanese honeysuckle.*** *People enjoy sucking the nectar from the base of flowers as do hummingbirds.*

*Lonicera japonica* **JAPANESE HONEYSUCKLE**
**Family:** *Caprifoliaceae*
**Zone:** 5a Evergreen Vine
**Flowering:** Spring and summer
**Fruiting:** Summer and autumn
**Size:** Vine to 20' or more

This Japanese native is more common than the Japanese manufactured automobiles. Since its introduction, the vine has become widespread over the entire eastern United States. It is a rampant grower in full sunlight and shade and seems to have no particular preference as to soil type. White flowers, turning yellow on the second day, are highly fragrant and are present during the entire growing season. Green solitary to clustered berries turn black in summer and fall.

**Comments:** This vigorously growing vine will engulf plants over which it spreads, resulting in the death of its support host. Managed properly and kept in bounds, the Japanese honeysuckle has many valuable landscape attributes, especially in the western part of the region.

*Lonicera sempervirens* **CORAL HONEYSUCKLE**
**Family:** *Caprifoliaceae*
**Zone:** 4a Evergreen Vine
**Flowering:** Spring and summer
**Fruiting:** Summer and autumn
**Size:** Vine to 20' or more

A tamer member of the honeysuckle vines with a much slower rate of growth, this native thrives in moist, fertile, slightly alkaline soils in full sunlight, but will tolerate most growing conditions. Flower production is reduced in partial shade. Orange-scarlet, trumpet-shaped flowers with yellow centers are two inches in size in terminal clusters. Heaviest flowering is in spring and summer with a few blossoms appearing in autumn. The orange to scarlet fruit, up to one-quarter inch in diameter, usually produced in clusters, is present in late summer and fall.

**Birds that feed on honeysuckles:** Hummingbirds, orchard oriole, and Northern oriole (nectar); Eastern bluebird, mockingbird, cedar waxwing, evening grosbeak, gray catbird, and hermit thrush.

**Comments:** Among the best vines for use on garden structures when a vine requiring low maintenance is needed. Reported to be a source of very high quality nectar.

*Fruit of Japanese (black) and coral (red) honeysuckle.*

**Coral honeysuckle.** *An absolute must for any hummingbird garden.*

*Malvaviscus arboreus* **GIANT TURK'S CAP**
**Family:** *Malvaceae* Shrubby Perennial
**Zone:** 8b
**Flowering:** Summer to frost
**Size:** 8' × 8'

Without winter protection, this rangy, semitropical shrub grows only in the Deep South. It thrives in fertile, well-drained soils, but will grow under most growing conditions, provided the plant receives full sunlight, preferably during the morning hours. It is well adapted to the stressful conditions of inner city gardens and old specimens are common on south-facing walls in these locations. This plant has relatively large heart-shaped leaves and drooping, bright scarlet, three-inch, tubular-shaped flowers with protruding centers.

**Comments:** In the northern part of the region, grow this perennial as a tub specimen very much like you would other tropicals, such as Chinese hibiscus.

***Giant Turk's cap.*** *This tropical can bloom twelve months of the year, when not injured by cold.*

*Malvaviscus arboreus* 'Drummondii' **TURK'S CAP**
**Family:** *Malvaceae* Perennial
**Zone:** 8a
**Flowering:** Summer
**Size:** 4' × 3'

A common, semiwoody perennial which has escaped cultivation in the western part of the region. It has an open, irregular form and will grow in alkaline soils in droughty locations. This species has small heart-shaped leaves and bright, red, upright, tubular flowers followed by small applelike, red fruits. Blooms may occur all year in frost-free areas.

**Birds that feed on Turk's caps:** Hummingbirds.

***Turk's cap.*** *Has been grown in Southern gardens for over a century and has escaped cultivation over much of the region.*

**Comments:** Turk's cap is an extremely tough plant for adverse growing conditions. Fruits look like small, red apples in summer and fall.

**Firecracker vine.** *An excellent plant for fall migrating hummingbirds. Pinch the bud and hear the "firecracker" pop.*

*Manettia cordifolia* **FIRECRACKER VINE**
**Family:** *Rubiaceae* Perennial Vine
**Zone:** 8b
**Flowering:** Summer and autumn
**Size:** Vine to 15'

This little-known, light, lacy-foliaged vine is well adapted to the lower South where it grows best in full sunlight and in a moderately fertile, well-drained soil. It is normally killed back to the ground in winter, but returns from a mass of fleshy roots in spring. Grow this vine on arbors, trellises, fences, and other landscape structures which provide support. An abundance of red, tubular-shaped flowers are present from late spring until frost. This vine flowers much more profusely as the days become shorter in late summer and fall.

**Birds:** Hummingbirds.

**Comments:** After the foliage is killed by cold temperatures, the vine should be cut back; even when it does not freeze, an annual winter pruning is desirable. Can be readily propagated from root cuttings.

*Monarda citriodora* **LEMON or HORSE MINT**
**Family:** *Labiatae*
**Zone:** 5b Perennial
**Flowering:** Spring and summer
**Size:** 4' × 2'

This tall-growing perennial of the mint family flourishes in most any well-drained soil in full sunlight to partial shade. It tolerates droughty conditions well and spreads rapidly under favorable growing conditions. Plants have aromatic leaves and produce clusters of rose-pink flowers in summer and autumn. There are a number of cultivated varieties of M. *didyma* (bee balm) and some of the finer ones are 'Cambridge Scarlet,' 'Croftway Pink,' 'Mrs. Perry' (red), and 'Panoramic' mixture.

**Birds:** Hummingbird.

**Comments:** For best performance, old, mature clumps should be dug and separated in late autumn. Discard the weak, inner sections of old clumps and save and replant the outer, more vigorous plants.

**Lemon or bee balm.** *There are many species of monarda, or bee balm, and most attract hummingbirds.*

**Virginia creeper.** *This is probably the most important vine that produces fruits eaten by birds.*

*Parthenocissus quinquefolia* **VIRGINIA CREEPER**
Deciduous Vine
**Family:** *Vitaceae*
**Zone:** 4b
**Fruiting:** Autumn
**Size:** Vine to 100' or more

This native vine grows over the entire region in natural and manmade landscapes. It thrives in moist soils in full sunlight to shade, and tolerates very stressful conditions. Virginia creeper is best known for its clinging qualities on walls, but grows on the trunks and in canopies of trees. The five-leaflet leaves distinguish this vine from poison ivy, which has three leaflets. The dark blue fruits, each about one-fourth inch in diameter, are produced in long clusters in early autumn.

**Birds:** Red-bellied, pileated, and red-headed woodpeckers; Eastern kingbird; great crested flycatcher; tufted titmouse; white-breasted nuthatch; mockingbird; brown thrasher; American robin; wood, hermit, and Swainson's thrushes; yellow-bellied sapsucker; gray catbird; northern flicker; Eastern bluebird; yellow-rumped warbler; red-eyed vireo; bay-breasted warbler; scarlet tanager; purple finch; starling; and fox sparrow.

**Comments:** Virginia creeper is very fast growing and invasive, but is pest free. It is highly drought tolerant, has handsome rosy red autumn foliage color, and produces large quantities of seeds over the entire region, making it an important source of food for many birds in early autumn.

*Pentas lanceolata* **PENTAS**
**Family:** *Rubiaceae* Herbaceous Perennial
**Zone:** 8b
**Flowering:** Spring and summer
**Size:** to 3'

This seldom grown, relatively tall-growing perennial performs best in full sunlight in fertile, well-drained soils, but tolerates a fairly broad range of growing conditions. The flowers are tubular, about one inch long arranged in close, clustered flower heads. Colors include white, red, and pink, but the red is reported to be the preference of hummingbirds.

**Birds:** Hummingbirds.

**Comments:** Flowers over a long period from spring until frost.

**Pentas.** *Butterflies and hummingbirds suck the nectar from the flowers.*

*Phytolacca americana* **POKEBERRY or POKEWEED**
**Family:** *Phytolaccaceae*
**Zone:** 5a Perennial
**Fruiting:** Summer and autumn
**Size:** 10' × 6'

Treated as an annual in the North where roots are often killed, it is a perennial in the lower South. Pokeberry is a rampant grower in most soils, but thrives in moist, fertile soils and is especially well adapted to woodland edges. The roots, which resemble horseradish, are poisonous. The young, tender, emerging leaves may be eaten as a salad green. Six-inch flower spikes give rise to purplish-black berries throughout the summer and fall until frost.

**Birds:** Eastern bluebird, mockingbird, American robin, gray catbird, Eastern kingbird, summer tanager, cedar waxwing, Swainson's thrush, white-throated sparrow, brown thrasher, red-bellied and red-headed woodpeckers, cardinal, mourning dove, and starling.

**Comments:** A highly attractive fruiting plant for a large number of birds. In colonial times, the fruit juice was used for dying fabrics.

**Pokeberry.** *Often in the weed category, but a widely distributed native that produces fruit eaten by many birds.*

**Blackberry.** *The blackberry and its close relative the dewberry are among the top bird foods in spring.*

*Rubus* sp. **BLACKBERRY AND DEWBERRY**
**Family:** *Rosaceae*
**Zone:** 2a Woody Rambler
**Fruiting:** Spring and summer
**Size:** Rambles to 20'

The blackberries and dewberries of North American origin are derived from native species. The cultivated varieties can not always be traced to their origins, because they are hybrids and cannot be classified according to species. Consequently members of this genus are widely distributed. They normally grow best in an open exposure in any average garden soil, but are tolerant of most growing conditions. Volunteer seedlings have naturalized over the entire region and will quickly engulf an open, unmanaged site. Early white flowers are followed by multiple-seeded fruits in spring. The black fruits, because of their sugar content, are a preferred food source of many birds.

**Birds:** Red-bellied and red-headed woodpeckers; Eastern kingbird; great crested flycatcher; blue jay; tufted titmouse; mockingbird; gray catbird; brown thrasher; American robin; wood, Swainson's and gray-cheeked thrushes; Eastern bluebird; cedar waxwing; white-eyed and red-eyed vireos; yellow-breasted chat; common grackle; orchard and northern orioles; summer and scarlet tanagers; cardinal; rose-breasted; blue and evening grosbeaks; indigo bunting; rufous-sided towhee; and white-throated and fox sparrows.

**Comments:** There are many cultivars of blackberries that produce fruits much larger than those found in nature. Under cultivation, canes must be cut to the ground annually after fruiting to prevent carry over of the double-blossom fungus disease.

## *Salvias*

**Family:** *Labiatae*

Most salvias are perennials or sub-shrubs in their native habitats, but many are grown as annuals over much of the South. In areas of the region that are relatively frost-free, salvias may attain a height of eight feet or more. Where they over winter, they usually become unsightly and will produce much more pleasing specimens when cut near the ground in early spring.

No other group of flowering perennials is more widely used by hummingbirds than are the salvias. Several species may be used in the same garden to give a wide variety of flower colors: white, pink, red, blue, and purple.

Salvias are tolerant of a wide range of soils, but grow best in slightly acid, well-drained soils. Salvias must have sun for best growth and flowering, however, several do reasonably well in partial

**Salvias or sages.** *Among the most important garden plants from which hummingbirds get nectar. Left to right: Mexican bush sage, Vanhoutte sage, forsythia sage, pineapple-scented sage, anise sage 'Purple Majesty.'*

shade for several hours each day. They will withstand drier growing conditions than most other flowering annuals and perennials. After having completed a heavy flush of growth and flowering, they generally become unattractive. A shearing at this time, along with a light fertilization and adequate moisture, will restore the plants to an attractive growth and flowering state.

*Salvia coccinea* **SCARLET SAGE**
**Size:** to 2' Perennial

The scarlet or Texas sage produces scarlet flowers and is a native of the region. It is reported to make satisfactory growth in alkaline soils.

Frost kills plants to the ground, but they quickly return in early spring.

'Lady in Red,' a recent introduction that is dwarf in growth habit, produces large quantities of flowers.

*Salvia Greggii* **AUTUMN or CHERRY SAGE**
**Size:** to 3' Perennial

Neither of its common names fits this plant. It starts flowering relatively early in spring and its flowers are more purplish than cherry red. This West Texas native requires good drainage and full sunlight, and thrives with little care.

*Salvia guaranitica* **ANISE SAGE**
**Size:** 3'–4' Perennial

This salvia from South America produces one-to two-inch-long dark blue to violet-blue flowers on tall stalks. It is grown as an annual in the mid-to upper South. *S. guaranitica* 'Purple Majesty' has a deep purple flower.

***Salvias.*** *Left to right: bog sage, Belize sage, Mexican sage, autumn (or cherry) sage.*

*Salvia leucantha* **MEXICAN BUSH SAGE**
**Size:** 3'–4' Perennial

A salvia with large, gray-green leaves that are pubescent below. It is probably the largest, but is also the most cold tender of the salvias. The violet-purple flowers are three-fourth inch long.

*Salvia splendens* **SCARLET SAGE**
**Size:** 2–8' Perennial

The most widely grown of the salvias, it thrives during the hot summer months in full sunlight and grows in most garden soils, provided they are well drained. There are both standard and dwarf varieties. While reds are the most popular colors in the dwarfs, other selections of the dwarf types include purple, white, and pink. A cultivar of this species that is exceptionally outstanding for flowering and hummingbird attraction is 'Red Hot Sally.'

**Birds that feed on Salvia:** Hummingbirds and orchard orioles.

**Comments:** Other species of salvia used to attract hummingbirds include Pineapple sage

*Scarlet sage, among the most widely grown garden salvias.*

(*S. elegans*) and Belize salvia (*S. gesnerifolia* x *guaranitica*), *S. madrensis* (Forsythia sage) with yellow flowers, Bog salvia (*S. uliginosa*) has blue flowers, *S. rutilans,* also known as *S. elegans,* has long scarlet flowers, *S. mexicana* (Mexican sage) has deep blue flowers, *S. mineata* has red flowers, and *S. Vanhouttei* (Vanhoutte sage) with purplish red flowers.

*Smilax* sp. **SOUTHERN SMILAX**
**Family:** *Liliaceae* Evergreen Vines
**Zone:** 6a
**Fruiting:** Autumn
**Size:** Vine to 40'

This genus includes several native evergreen vines, some of which are found in all parts of the region. They are normally high climbing and hidden by the foliages of the host trees until leaf-drop in late autumn. The vines grow in full sunlight to partial shade and make excellent cover for garden structures such as arbors and trellises. Berries that are one-fourth to one-half inch in diameter are produced on the large, draping, massive vines during fall and winter. Thorny stems can be hazardous.

**Birds:** Red-bellied woodpecker; mockingbird; gray catbird; brown thrasher; American robin; hermit, Swainson's, and gray-cheeked thrushes; Eastern bluebird; cedar waxwing; common grackle; white-throated and fox sparrows; and cardinal.

**Comments:** The lustrous, dark green, shiny leaves which are pale-green on the lower surfaces make an excellent cut foliage. Sarsaparilla is produced from the dried roots of several tropical American species.

***Southern smilax.*** *Fruit is seldom seen because it is borne on vines high in the treetops.*

*Spigelia marilandica* **INDIAN PINK**
**Family:** *Loganiaceae* Herbaceous Perennial
**Zone:** 5b
**Flowering:** Spring
**Size:** to 2'

This native perennial occurs over the entire region, but is not normally abundant. Usually found growing in small colonies in fertile, moist soils and full sunlight to partial shade. Red, trumpet-shaped flowers with yellow throats are produced in terminal, elongated, curved clusters on one side of the stems. This delicate wildflower blooms from April to June.

**Birds:** Hummingbirds

**Comments:** Indian pinks combine well with other small perennials in detail garden design, but they cannot compete with aggressively growing plants.

***Indian pink.*** *This native perennial wildflower merits more use by gardeners.*

*Tropaeolum majus* **GARDEN NASTURTIUM**
**Family:** *Tropaeolaceae* Annual
**Flowering:** Spring
**Size:** 12' to 10'

***Garden nasturtium.*** *Enjoyed by hummingbirds; people enjoy flowers in salads.*

Wild nasturtiums grow from Chile north to Mexico. The hybrid strains developed from these vary in height from the dwarfs, which seldom exceed 12 inches, to the climbers, which may attain a length of 10 or more feet. Some of the trailing varieties make excellent hanging basket specimens. Flowers are about two inches across and blossoms come in a wide variety of colors: white, yellow, orange, scarlet, cerise, mahogany, and deep red. Nasturtiums will thrive in most garden soils, but flower poorly in those that are very fertile. Plant them where they receive six or more morning hours of sunlight each day, but in shade near midday. They do not like hot weather and begin to die out after night temperatures consistently above 65 degrees F.

**Birds:** Hummingbirds.

**Comments:** For best flowering, plant in a relatively poor soil and get the seeds in the ground as soon as danger of freezes are over. However, plants will tolerate a light frost. Flowers are sometimes used in leafy vegetable salads.

*Vitis* sp. **GRAPES**
**Family:** *Vitaceae* Deciduous Vines
**Zone:** 6a
**Fruiting:** Summer and autumn
**Size:** Vine to 60'

Native and introduced climbing vines grown for their fruits which are used fresh to make juice, jelly, and wine. They may be grown on trellises, fences, and arbors. Grapes thrive in sandy, well-drained soils in full sunlight to partial shade. Grapes have been used to cover garden structures since Colonial times. Fruit sizes vary from one-fourth inch for some of the natives up to one inch for some of the improved muscadine types. The color of fruit varies from green to copper to black. Many kinds of grapes have a high sugar content that is sought by birds.

**Birds:** Mourning dove; red-bellied and red-headed woodpeckers; Eastern kingbird; blue jay; great crested flycatcher; tufted titmouse; mockingbird; gray catbird; brown thrasher; American robin; wood, hermit, gray-cheeked, and Swainson's thrushes; Eastern bluebird; red-eyed vireo; yellow-breasted chat; house and fox sparrows; orchard and northern orioles; scarlet and summer tanagers; cardinal; purple finch; American goldfinch; and rufous-sided towhee.

**Comments:** The muscadine (*V. rotundifolia*) is a very important native grape in the deep South where few other bunch grapes grow. Established grape plants must be pruned annually to maintain fruitfulness and the desired growth habit.

Other plants that are excellent bird food include poison ivy (*Rhus radicans*) and pepper vine (*Ampelopsis aborea*). Both of these are native vines of wild areas and have serious landscape deficiencies. **Poison ivy** produces white, waxy berries that ripen in fall and persist into winter and these are relished by many species of birds. However, most people are highly allergic to poison ivy which causes a rash that can become a serious medical problem. For this reason, we can not recommend the planting of poison ivy in residential landscapes. **Pepper vine** produces berries that are good bird food and is excellent browse material for deer. It is a rampant grower and can engulf garden plants in a year or two. In addition, it produces tremendous numbers of berries which produce volunteer plants to further spread this vine. Because of its quick invasiveness by seedlings it is not recommended for home gardens.

There are many, many plants that are nectar sources for hummingbirds and a presentation of these would require a book of considerable length. Some of these may suit a particular landscape need such as a particular need for color, texture, form, or seasonal interest.

**Grapes.** *A favorite of many fruit-eating birds. There are many cultivars that can be grown in the region.*

*Blue Jay (Cyanocitta cristata) by H. Douglas Pratt*

# Garden Accessories for Birds

There are three groups of garden accessories that are especially important for attracting birds to your garden. These groups are feeding stations with supplemental food, water features, and shelter/cover, including bird houses.

## *Feeding Stations and Food*

Feeding is the easiest and simplest way to bring a variety of birds within easy viewing range. The need to feed birds may be more for the benefit of humans than for the birds themselves. However, in the United States, one-third of U.S. households feed wild birds. Over thirty-seven million persons are engaged in purchasing seed for birds. Today one can find commercially prepared seed in supermarkets, hardware stores, and garden centers. Even convenience stores are providing a ready supply. On an annual basis Americans are spending $1.1 billion for bird seed. Over thirty thousand tons of seeds are dispensed annually from at least twelve million backyard feeders. More people feed wild birds than hunt and fish combined. This does not belittle these other outdoor recreational activities, but probably should cause fish and wildlife agencies to rethink the importance of watchable wildlife.

*A squirrel-proof feeder sitting in a low planting adjacent to a patio.*

*Hummingbird feeder containing clear sugar water. Coloring is not needed.*

Since a feeding station is just like any other garden accessory in relationship to landscape design, we must consider it as a part of the overall design. That is, it should meet the requirements of the birds as well as the design of the rest of the garden. The station should fit in. Your landscape may have existing features that can be used in the design of the station. Look for outcrops of rocks, tree stumps, fallen logs, fences or other features that can be used or enhanced. Emphasize what is special about your landscape.

Selecting the specific feeder and locating it in your garden are the two most important considerations in the design process. The feeder should be located so that it adds to the composition of the garden. Think of it in visual terms as being the same as locating a piece of sculpture. The bird feeder becomes a kinetic feature in the garden. Many considerations must be made in determining the location of the feeding stations.

In contemporary garden design, a strong relationship between indoors and outdoors has been a desirable component to the design. The location of a window is the normal structural element that facilitates this relationship. Placing the bird feeding station outside a window allows

*A host of house finches feeding on a post feeder, which is reported to be squirrel proof when placed in an open area.*

you to have the greatest benefit for your efforts. The closer the feeder is to the window the better view you should have of the birds.

Windows can cause some problem in relationship to birds. Unfortunately many birds fly into glass windows and are dazed or killed. It appears that the birds are seeing reflections of lawn, woodlands, or open sky and are not aware of the danger. Also, territorial birds may see reflections of themselves and try to drive the "other" birds off. If possible, adjust the angle of the glass to reduce these reflections. Tilting the glass five to six degrees downward may help. Other aids in preventing window accidents are to hang stained glass or other obstructions inside the window. If the problem is bad, consider a screen or net in front of the window.

Large feeding stations require more visual attention than smaller ones, such as suet feeders on a tree. In relationship to attracting the most birds, you want a variety of sizes, locations, and feeding types. A large shelf feeder requires the most design attention. This should be located so you can see the birds easily. They need to have a space around the feeder that is appropriate and in proportion to the feeder. Style and color of the feeder may be important to the overall design, but remember, it must also meet the function of feeding the birds. Bright colors may not be appropriate, but any color can be subdued in its intensity and blended into a natural color. Style can also vary without having an impact on the function. A well-proportioned feeder will always fit. There are many well-designed commercial feeding stations available, but there are also a lot of commercial stations that will look just plain out-of-place in your landscape.

In placing your feeding station, keep several factors in mind. You want to bring the birds to where you can see them and get the most enjoyment from your efforts. This generally means

*Feeders and houses should be placed where they can be viewed from indoors.*

*Mourning doves and grosbeak feeding on a shelf feeder.*

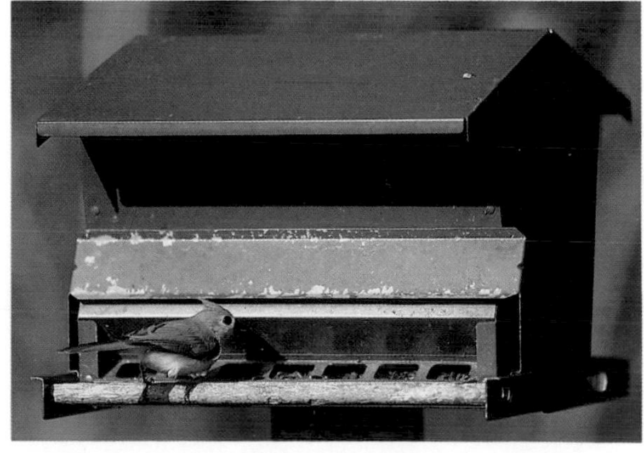

*A commercial feeder which closes mechanically to protect the food supply from squirrels and large birds.*

close to the house, but that is not always the case. A small hummingbird feeder may fit under the eaves of the house, but if it is a couple of feet further away, the bird may be in the sunshine and all its colors would show more brightly.

Consider the surface of the ground under your feeder. Hard surfaces are easy to clean and allow you to get to the feeder and fill it as well as clean it. Grass is good. The lawn mower will take care of any seeds that germinate. If you locate the feeder over ground cover, you will want to get the ground cover established before you site the feeder because inevitably a lot of weeds will appear. One good surface is a covering of fallen leaves. This is especially appealing to ground-feeding birds that will go through all the leaves to find what they want. If you use leaves, it probably is a good idea to keep a bag of leaves available to restock the area or it will soon become bare dirt.

Think about the background plantings. You will want both evergreens and deciduous branches for birds to perch on while waiting their turn at the station. Cover is needed for the birds in case a predator appears. If you are interested in bird photography, you can design the station with this in mind. Considerations here would include backgrounds and the focal distances of your lenses. As stated earlier, the space around the feeding station should be in the right proportion to the station. This is done easily by the placement of the background plants nearby.

The type of feeding station you are locating will also affect the design. Stations can be placed in several groups or types: platform/shelf feeders, hopper seed dispensers, suet/peanut butter feeders, nectar feeders, ground feeders, and fruit/nut holders. Each of these types comes in many variations of design. Many can be both pole mounted or hung by a wire. Each type and mounting technique will help determine the amount of space and other sitting requirement appropriate. Since this is basically a plant book a word should be given about attaching feeders to living trees. Nails or hooks can become embedded in a tree branch over time and may provide an entrance into the plant for disease. However, this is better than wrapping bare wire around a branch without protection since this might girdle the tree in time. If you do attach feeders or bird houses to trees, remember to protect the trees and to service them annually.

Variety is the most important consideration, from the view of the birds, in setting up a feeding station. Since different birds have different preferences, the best way to attract them is to give them choices of food, location, and cover for protection while they are eating.

Although we want to provide the birds with a variety of foods, certain foods are better in attracting the birds we want. Aelred D. Geis of the U.S. Fish and Wildlife Service conducted research on bird seed and his 1980 publication on this subject became one of the most popular papers ever released by the Service. Geis's study revealed that the birds were especially attracted to sunflower seed, white proso millet, and niger (thistle) seed. Personal observations support these findings.

Sunflower (*Helianthus annuus*) seed will attract the greatest variety and most number of visits of any of the three recommended seeds. Cardinals, chickadees, titmice, and finches are among the perch-feeding birds which prefer sunflower seed. Four types of sunflower seed are generally available. They are the large gray shelled seed, the smaller black striped seed, black oilseed, and hulled sunflower seed made from the other three. Since the introduction of the black oilseed, previously used only for its oil, the choice for birds is clear. The two smaller black seeds are the best, with the black oilseed being the one seed most attractive to birds. The smaller seed

*Examples of seeds commercially available for feeding birds. 1. black oil sunflower, 2. striped sunflower, 3. sunflower hearts, 4. proso millet, 5. Siberian millet. 6. safflower, 7. corn, 8. cracked corn, 9. fine corn, 10. thistle (niger).*

also has more seeds to the pound and thereby will feed more birds.

The hulled sunflower seed is the most attractive food for the American goldfinch. Its next favorite food at feeders is niger seed. Hulled seed is also attractive to white-throated sparrows. Few other birds like the hulled seed. However, the hulled seed may be a good choice for one who wishes to avoid the accumulation of hulls under feeders.

Since many birds like the sunflower seeds so much, you will find it best to have some of your feeders filled only with this seed. One reason for this is that in a mix many birds will discard or waste all other seed in their effort to get to the sunflower seeds.

Birds attracted to sunflower seed include chickadees, evening grosbeaks, tufted titmice, blue jays, American goldfinches, house finches, purple finches, and cardinals. Forty other species, including wild turkey, nuthatches, scrub jay, black-headed grosbeak, and downy and hairy woodpeckers, also prize this seed.

White proso millet (*Panicum miliaceum*) is one of two color types, red and white, of proso millet. The white type is preferred especially by ground-feeding birds such as white-throated sparrows and mourning doves. The hard seed coat of the millet resists swelling when wet and is therefore easier to dispense in hopper feeders, since it tends not to clog the feeder.

Birds attracted to white proso millet include tree sparrow, song sparrow, brown-headed cowbird, dark-eyed junco, house sparrow, mourning dove, white-throated sparrow, northern bobwhite, painted bunting, dickcissel, rufous-sided towhee, and several species of waterfowl such as mallard redhead, Northern shoveler, American widgeon, and green-winged teal.

Niger (*Guizotia abyssinica*) seed is often called "thistle" seed although it is not even closely related to the familiar prickly thistle and is imported to this country. Niger seed especially attracts American goldfinches, which eat this seed almost as readily as sunflower seed. Although the niger seed is often expensive, its very

*This three-tubed feeder containing thistle (niger) seed attracts multitudes of American goldfinches.*

small size gives you a lot of seeds to the pound. Special feeders have been designed to dispense this tiny black seed with little waste. These feeders have small holes. Larger billed birds like house sparrows cannot gain access to the seed without enlarging the hole.

Birds attracted to niger seed include American goldfinch, purple finch, house finch, redpoll, pine siskin, mourning dove, song sparrow, white-throated sparrow, and dark-eyed junco. Although the idea of seed mixes supports the concept of offering birds a variety of foods, the commercial mixes may not always be your best buy even though the price may seem lower than the price of single seed. Because of the competitive nature of commercial bird seed mixes, some of the ingredients in typical mixes are not that attractive to the birds themselves. Some mixes contain seeds that are attractive to birds that are considered by some to be undesirable. For example, oat groats, a frequent ingredient in mixes, is relished by starlings. This material also will often become moldy. Another frequent ingredient in seed mixes is milo, which has been found to be unattractive to birds. Other ingredients in mixes may be more appealing to humans than to birds. The little pointy ends of peanuts known as "hearts," which are discarded by the manufacturers of peanut butter, are frequently found in mixes and smell good to humans when they open the bag, but are again more attractive to starlings than other birds. The use of most commercially prepared mixes is an inefficient way to feed birds. Much of the material is wasted because of lack of interest by the birds themselves.

Both suet and peanut butter are high-protein food supplements for birds. They are eaten by many species of birds, including insect-eating birds, such as woodpeckers. Feed suet to birds whole or process it by melting it and then letting it resolidify. You will also find commercial suet-

*Suet provides a high-calorie food needed by birds in winter. The red-bellied woodpecker is eating from a feeder designed to contain suet in winter and peanut butter and other mixes in summer.*

seed cakes are widely available. However, the mixture of seed and suet is somewhat counterproductive because it attracts both seed and suet eaters to the same feeder. Suet can also be mixed with peanut butter in various combinations. Since suet becomes rancid in temperatures above 70° F, it is best used at your winter feeding stations. Of all the winter foods, few can match suet for producing the body heat birds need to stay warm. Peanut butter can be used in the summer and is probably best mixed in proportions of one cup peanut butter to five cups of cornmeal or it may be used with equal parts of flour, cornmeal, and oil (vegetable oil or lard—again, in order to avoid it's getting rancid in warm temperatures, only put out what can be consumed by the birds in one day, approximately a golfball-sized amount).

Many insect-eating birds—especially woodpeckers—like suet/peanut butter, as do other birds that include chickadees, nuthatches, titmice, and blue jays. Even seed-eating cardinals are attracted to this high-protein food.

Also, try supplying fruits such as apples, oranges, grapefruits, bananas, grapes, and raisins for the birds. You will find that these are favorites for many tropical migrants like orioles, tanagers and warblers. Fruit must be provided in small pieces or attached to the feeder in some way so that a large bird will not take it all away at one time. You will find that red-bellied and hairy woodpeckers like slices of apple and mockingbirds like sectioned grapefruit.

Nectar and sugar water feeders are just what is needed to attract hummingbirds and orioles. Granulated sugar should be dissolved in water in the ratio of one part sugar to four parts water. This mixture can be used without adding any red color. If you like the looks of red water put the solution in a red container. Orioles will often go to a hummingbird feeder and empty it in no time. To discourage this, provide the orioles with their own feeder. A poultry water dispenser, which is nothing more than a mason jar turned upside down to release water into a circular trough, filled with sugar water will be popular with these birds.

Wintertime is the most common season for feeding birds. Many believe that it is necessary to provide birds with food at this time or they will starve. The truth is, if we do not feed the birds they will go elsewhere and may find a bountiful supply of natural food or seed supplied by a neighbor. One of the reasons for planting our garden with plants that are attractive to birds is so that the birds will have food if we neglect our feeding chores or go on vacation. Conventional wisdom tells us not to stop feeding once it is started. It is not necessary; but you may have more birds if they know they can depend on your station.

Traditionally winter has been the time to feed birds but summer is becoming more and more popular. As we realize that the food is not necessary, but a pleasure for ourselves, why not extend this pleasure to the summer, especially if it allows

*Simple watering and feeding station as viewed from inside a house.*

us more opportunity to view birds while it gives our gardens more color and activity. Winter may continue to be the most popular bird feeding season, but many people are discovering the benefits of summer feeding.

## *Water Features*

Surprisingly, water is often forgotten when setting up a bird garden. Birds really do not need much water, but a little can make a big difference. In the southwestern part of our area, water may be more attractive to birds than food. Birds get much of their water needs from food, yet when we see birds bathing or drinking we know just how much they both need and like water. Birds such as vireos and warblers who are seldom attracted to feeding stations may visit our garden water features.

*An assemblage of driftwood and stone made into a watering station at the Caroline Dormon Nature Preserve in Saline, Louisiana.*

*The sound of water dripping from one tier to the next attracts birds.*

Since most birdbaths are as large as shelf feeders, they require at least as much attention in their design and location. Actually most water features require more design consideration because they can be large in size and have many more technical requirements. Availability of both water and electricity may be necessary in the design. In gardens that are designed without birds as a central theme, water features can be prominent accents to the garden. With a little extra attention to detail these same designs can be made to appeal to birds. One area that makes a difference is the depth of water. Garden birds rarely want water deeper than two and one-half inches. However you can have a water feature deeper than this if you also provide a shallow area and a ledge to perch on.

In Louisiana, a favorite garden water feature is an old sugar kettle converted into a fountain. The kettles are much too deep for most birds, but the addition of a shelf or even plants like water lettuce that birds can stand on, make this traditional feature attractive to birds.

Certainly, a water feature should be appropriate to the space that it is occupying. A commercial ceramic birdbath may be the simplest solution for providing water. However, some of the birdbaths are inappropriate for bird use. Some are just too deep. They need rock islands installed. Other commercial baths look leggy and out of proportion to the rest of the garden. Often these baths look fine if the pedestal is just buried in the ground a bit to reduce the height. The idea of providing water off the ground, where you would normally find it, is to provide some extra protection from attack by cats.

Just turning on the garden sprinkler can be a real attraction to birds. Save the watering chores to a time when you can watch. You may have some surprising results. Have the sprinkler where you can see it and where it is watering the trees and shrubs that make up your garden edges. Not only the sight of water, but also the sound of moving water of all types is very important in attracting birds. In areas where rainwater is scarce, water can be collected and stored for later use. Rain falling on patios, driveways, and other paved areas can be drained to storage bins and then used when it will be most appreciated by the birds.

*A small, inexpensive, simple shell bird bath.*

*Water-conserving sprinkler system designed specifically to attract birds for drinking and bathing at the AmeriFlora '92 in Columbus, Ohio.*

*A bird house in a planting of wildflowers with the hole oriented to the open space.*

Dripping water or the sound of water moving over a rock is most effective. Another way to make a small amount of water go a long way is by using a mister. This will provide a very fine spray. This can be used by itself or in combination with other features such as the standard ceramic birdbath. Remember that water is needed all year round. It may be more difficult in the winter when it freezes, but it is needed. Electrical warming devices are commercially available to prevent the water freezing.

Where space permits, larger garden pools can be designed into the garden. These pools can do the whole job of providing water or you can still have the smaller birdbath in addition to the pool.

## Shelter and Bird Houses

The third area of garden accessories important for attracting birds is that which emphasizes shelter for the birds. Our garden plants may be the best feature providing cover and nesting area, but manmade bird houses also merit con-

*An assortment of birdhouses attached to trees in a naturalistic landscape.*

sideration. Many fine bird houses are commercially available, but like feeders and birdbaths they may not fit your garden design. Again selection is important. You can find many designs that are more attractive to people than to birds.

The building of bird houses or feeders can be an important family project. It may be a child's first lesson in the importance of birds or in the use of tools. Never build a generic bird house. Only build houses for specific birds. See the chart on bird house dimensions, for details. A bird house built for any bird will probably end up housing no birds. The only birds that can really be attracted to using a house are cavity nesters. A few other birds can be encouraged to use shelves or baskets.

Locate the houses as shown in Table 1. If you are lucky and have a lot of property, you may get several different species nesting in your garden.

*Recycled milk cartons and similar containers make serviceable bird houses, such as for this prothonotary warbler.*

*A simple, easy-to-construct house made of weathered cypress, designed to specifically attract Eastern bluebirds.*

Remember that most cavity-nesting birds, with the exception of purple martins, are territorial, so you will not get more than one family of a specific bird in a small garden. The other exception to this one-species rule in small gardens are wrens. The male wren likes to build more than one nest so that the female can choose. Several wren houses would be appropriate in a given garden.

The purple martin house is becoming very popular. This multicellular nesting box or gourd collection can attract a very acrobatic insect-eater that is fascinating to watch. If you are building or buying a house, consider having all the holes on one side facing your favorite window so you can see all the birds. Also it is most convenient if the house is located on a telescoping pole so that the house can be raised and lowered for cleaning as needed. If you use a pole that is hinged you cannot lower the house when it is occupied. Martin houses should have perches and low hole openings.

If you have a very large property or are participating in the construction of a bluebird trail, you may want more than one bluebird house. It would be convenient if each box had a number or other designation so that it could be referred to easily. Note that bluebird boxes do not have perches in front of the door. This is to help prevent entry by starlings and sparrows. In fact, most houses do not have perches for just this reason.

*One of many designs for purple martins, which like to live in colonies.*

The construction of a brush pile in the garden will attract wrens and many ground-feeding birds such as brown thrashers. It is actually more than a heap of brush; it is a pile of sticks built on a foundation that lifts the small brush off the ground. The brush pile may not be appropriate if the design of your garden is very formal. However if you are designing a wild garden it fits in quite well.

| Species | Floor of cavity | Depth of cavity | Entrance above floor | Diameter of entrance | Height above ground |
|---|---|---|---|---|---|
| Carolina wren | 4" × 4" | 6"–8" | 4"–6" | 1½" | 6'–10' |
| Carolina chickadee | 4" × 4" | 8"–10" | 6"–8" | 1⅛" | 6'–15' |
| Tufted titmouse | 4" × 4" | 8"–10" | 6"–8" | 1¼" | 6'–15' |
| Eastern bluebird | 5" × 5" | 8" | 6" | 1½" | 5'–10' |
| Purple martin | 6" × 6" | 6" | 1" | 2½" | 15'–20' |
| House finch | 6" × 6" | 6" | 4" | 2" | 8'–12' |
| Crested flycatcher | 6" × 6" | 8"–10" | 6"–8" | 2" | 8'–20' |
| Red-headed woodpecker | 6" × 6" | 12"–15" | 9"–12" | 2" | 12'–20' |
| Prothonotary warbler | 4" × 4" | 6" | 4" | 1⅜" | 4'–12' |

*Table 1. Dimensions of nesting boxes for some species of birds.*
*Adapted from D. Daniel Boone, Homes for Birds, Conservation Bulletin 14, U.S. Fish and Wildlife Service, 1979.*

*Black-chinned Hummingbird* (Archilochus alexandri) *by John P. O'Neill*

# Some Common Myths about Southern Birds

J. V. Remsen, Jr.

1. "Robins are a sign of spring." Although the American robin breeds throughout the South, it is actually much more common here in *winter* than at other times of the year. In fact, when one *stops* seeing big numbers of robins in the Gulf Coast region, usually in March, that is a good sign that spring has begun. When the first major cold fronts strike the region in November, robins begin to arrive in large numbers, with flocks of hundreds often seen passing overhead in the early morning. Thus, the arrival of robins signifies the arrival of *winter*. Contributing to the misconception, at least in the Baton Rouge area, is that when robins first arrive, they feed mainly in the forest canopy on fruits of the hackberry and Virginia creeper and thus are not as conspicuous as they are late in winter, when depletion of these favored fruits forces them into suburban

*Dr. J. V. Remsen, Jr., is an ornithologist and Curator of the Museum of Natural Science at LSU. He is a native of Colorado and received his Ph.D. at the University of California—Berkeley.

gardens for ornamental fruits and lawn worms. Almost every year in February or March, local media report the "first" robins have been sighted and that "Spring must be on its way." One wonders why no one noticed the large numbers of robins feeding conspicuously along grassy road medians on cold January days!

2. "If you don't take down your hummingbird feeders in fall, you'll keep the hummingbirds from flying south for the winter." With statements like this printed in the instructions for some popular brands of hummingbird feeders, it is no surprise that this misconception is so widespread. One wonders why the feeder manufacturers didn't bother to consult a biologist about this. As with most migratory birds, the migrations of ruby-throated hummingbirds are almost certainly triggered by changes in day length, which in turn triggers releases of the hormones that allow them to store fat for fuel and that stimulate them to migrate. Therefore, removal of food supplies that the birds have been using to accumulate reserves of fat before migrating could conceivably reduce the birds' chances of leaving on time. Those who have left their feeders out in fall have found that the vast majority of ruby-throated hummingbirds leave when they are supposed to, in September and October, regardless of the presence of the food; the only way to *prevent* a healthy bird from migrating would be to cage it. Those few individuals that do remain are probably sick or injured birds that cannot leave; feeders maintained through the winter give these individuals a chance of recovering and surviving, as well as provide a food source for the several species of hummingbirds from the western United States and Mexico that are found in small numbers in winter through much of the Gulf Coast area. Over the last three decades, many hundreds if not thousands of hummingbirds have wintered successfully at feeders in the Gulf Coast area. Only during record-breaking cold winters has there been evidence of hummingbird deaths, and even then, many if not most hummingbirds survived.

3. "If you don't supply hummingbirds with proteins in addition to sugar water, they won't be able to survive the winter." Yes, hummingbirds need protein in their diet, but they evidently find enough insects through the winter that this is not a problem. As noted above, large numbers of hummingbirds have wintered successfully in the region. Some people seem to think that even in summer they must supply protein additives to their sugar water. This is completely unnecessary. Hummingbirds are capable of finding enough insects and tiny spiders on their own; in fact, studies have shown that most hummingbird stomachs are packed with insects.

4. "If you want hummingbirds at your feeder, you have to color the solution with red food coloring." Red color definitely attracts hummingbirds, more so than other colors, and so the plastic portions of most feeders are red. Although red food color in the solution might

make the feeder even more conspicuous to the hummingbirds, it is not necessary, especially once the feeder develops a clientele. The color of the solution itself is irrelevant. The birds probably can't see the color of the solution at their bill tip, and even if they could, it probably makes no difference to them. Nectar itself is colorless. Hummingbirds do visit flowers of virtually any color, if the flower provides an adequate nectar reward.

5. "The first purple martin to arrive are 'scouts' that inform the rest of the population concerning suitability of nesting conditions." There is no evidence for this anthropomorphic interpretation of the early arrival of individuals of this species. As far as is known, the first birds to arrive do not return south to the "main" population, which would be a highly altruistic act with no known counterpart in bird behavior.

6. "That's the biggest (pick any species) I've ever seen!" In contrast to other vertebrates, birds have "determinate" growth, meaning that young birds reach adult size at an early stage, usually as soon as independent of parental care, and do not continue to grow substantially in size thereafter. Furthermore, individual variation in size within a bird population is typically small and not noticeable to the human eye; usually only rulers and scales can detect the small differences in size among individuals of the same population. Thus, claims of a particular individual being noticeably large is usually the product of imagination or optical illusion. On the other hand, in some species the differences in size between males and females is noticeable, with males being larger, except in most hawks, falcons, owls, and a few other groups.

7. "Birds migrate to escape the cold." Although many birds leave northerly areas in winter, for the most part this is not because the birds cannot endure the cold itself, but because cold weather lowers food availability, especially of insects, or because freezing temperatures or snow conditions prevent access to food supplies. The birds themselves can often survive the cold temperatures, at least up to a point, as shown by the many cases in which an individual of a migratory species that normally winters much farther south remains behind, probably because of sickness or injury, and winters successfully at northern latitudes when it finds a feeder stocked with suitable food.

8. "Cats belong outside—it's natural." Although this myth doesn't refer directly to birds, it certainly has an extremely important negative effect on bird populations. Not only have pet cats been domesticated for thousands of years, but the original stock is also from the Eastern Hemisphere, not here, the Western Hemisphere. The only small cat native to the South, the bobcat, is substantially larger than a house cat and is in a different genus. Estimates of the numbers of birds killed each year in the United States by house cats range from to 50 million to 1.5 billion, an enormous drain on bird populations. Because most birds

benefit gardens by controlling many insect populations, cats that kill birds thus make more work for the gardener. Lizards and frogs, also voracious consumers of garden insects, are also killed by house cats in even greater numbers. Those who are truly concerned about their cats' health and safety should follow the advice of veterinarians and others by never letting them go outside.

9. "Parent birds desert their young if they smell human scent on the nest or nestling." Most birds are thought to have a relatively poor sense of smell. There is no evidence that they can detect human scent, and even if they could, it is unlikely that this would cause them to desert the nest. Nevertheless, there *is* an important reason why nestlings, nests, or anywhere in the vicinity of the nest should not be touched: mammals such as cats, opossums, raccoons, skunks, rats, and squirrels that eat eggs and nestlings may investigate human scent, and so a human may inadvertently lead a predator to a nest. The only reason to touch an active nest is to replace a nestling that has been knocked out of the nest. But the nestling must be so young that it cannot stand up—see the next item below.

10. "Baby birds that can't fly and are found out of the nest have been abandoned by the parents." Many people naturally want to help a flightless baby bird found out of the nest. If the bird *can* stand up, then it is likely that it has either fledged a few days prematurely, or perhaps was knocked out of the nest by a storm or predator. In some species, leaving the nest before being capable of flying is probably natural. In any case, it is best to leave the bird where it is. It is highly unlikely that the parents have abandoned the young. The parents undoubtedly know where the baby is, even if you don't see them—they are probably hunting nearby for food to bring to the baby. The best chance for the survival of the young bird is to let the parents continue to feed it until it can fly. If a person takes the baby away, its chances for survival are extremely low. Feeding a young bird enough food of the appropriate type is a tricky, time-consuming task. Even those experienced with feeding baby birds at rehabilitation centers may have difficulty raising a young bird. Even if raised successfully to the point that it can fly, a young bird released into the wild, without its parents to teach it how to find food and avoid predators has an extremely low probability of surviving more than a few days. Life is hazardous for young birds; even fledglings trained by their parents suffer high mortality, often around seventy-five percent, during their first year. Finally, special permits are required from the U.S. Fish and Wildlife Service to retain any native birds in captivity.

If one finds a bird so young that it *cannot* stand up, it probably has been or will be abandoned by the parents unless it can be replaced in the nest. If it cannot be replaced, then its only real chance for survival is to be delivered to a local bird rehabilitation center or to someone with extensive experience in, time for, and permits for raising nestlings.

# Bibliography


American Ornithologists' Union. *Check-List of North American Birds.* Prepared by the Committee on Classification and Nomenclature of the American Ornithologists' Union, 1983.

Barnes, I. R. "Planting for Birds." In *Landscaping for Birds.* Edited by S. A. Briggs. 2-10. Washington, D. C.: Audubon Naturalist Society of the Central Atlantic States, Inc., 1973.

Brooks, John. *The Country Garden.* New York: Crown Publishers, Inc., 1987.

Brooks, John. *The Small Garden.* New York: Gallery Books, 1990.

Bull, John, and John Ferrand, Jr. *The Audubon Society Field Guide to North American Birds. Eastern Region.* New York: Alfred A. Knopf, 1977.

Caillet, Marie, and Joseph K. Mertzweiller. *The Louisiana Iris.* Waco, Texas: Texas Gardener Press, 1988.

Chapman, Frank M. *Handbook of Birds of Eastern North America.* New York: Dover Publications, Inc., 1966.

Collins, H. H., and N. Boyajian. *Familiar Garden Birds of America.* New York: Harper and Row, 1965.

Davison, V. E. *Attracting Birds: From the Prairies to the Atlantic.* New York: Thomas Y. Crowell Co., 1967.

DeGraaf, Richard M., and Gretchen W. Witman. *Trees, Shrubs, and Vines for Attracting Birds. A Manual for Northeast U.S.* Amherst, Massachusetts: University of Massachusetts Press, 1979.

Dutton, Joan Parry. *Plants of Colonial Williamsburg.* Williamsburg, Virginia: The Colonial Williamsburg Foundation, 1979.

Feltwell, John, and Neil Odenwald. *Live Oak Splendor.* Dallas, Texas: Taylor Publishing Company, 1992.

Farrand, Jr., John, ed. *The Audubon Society Master Guide to Birding.* New York: Alfred A. Knopf, 1983.

Gude, G. "Shrubs Attractive to Birds." In *Landscaping for Birds.* Edited by S. A. Briggs. 25-32. Washington, D. C.: Audubon Naturalist Society of the Central Atlantic States, Inc., 1973.

Hobhouse, Penelope. *Garden Style.* Boston: Little, Brown and Co., 1988.

Jones, J. O. *Where the Birds Are. A Guide To All 50 States and Canada.* New York: William Morrow and Company, Inc., 1990.

Kress, Stephen W. *The Aubudon Society Guide to Attracting Birds.* New York: Charles Scribner's Sons, 1985.

Longenecker, G. W., and R. Ellarson. *Landscape Plants that Attract Birds.* Madison, Wisconsin: University of Wisconsin Extension Bulletin G1609, 1973.

Lowery, Jr., George H. *Louisiana Birds.* Baton Rouge, Louisiana: Louisiana Wildlife and Fisheries Commission, Louisiana State University Press, 1960.

Martin, A. C., H. S. Zim, and A. L. Nelson. *American Wildlife and Plants.* New York: Dover Publishing, Inc., 1951.

Mason, E. A. *One, Two, Three.* Lincoln, Massachusetts: Massachusetts Audubon Society, 1965.

McKenny, M. *Birds in the Garden and How to Attract Them.* New York: Royal and Hitchock, 1939.

National Geographic Society. *Field Guide to Birds of North America.* Washington, D.C.: The National Geographic Society, 1987.

Newfield, Nancy L. *Louisiana's Hummingbirds.* Baton Rouge, Louisiana: Louisiana Department of Wildlife and Fisheries, Louisiana Natural Heritage Program, 1991.

Odenwald, Neil, and James Turner. *Identification, Selection and Use of Southern Plants.* Baton Rouge, Louisiana: Claitor's Publishing Divisions, 1987.

O'Neill, John V. "Bird Seed Expert." *Bird Watcher's Digest* 11, no. 5 (May/June 1989). 47-51.

Peterson, Roger Tory. *A Field Guide to the Birds East of the Rockies.* Boston: Houghton Mifflin Company, 1991.

Petit, T. S. *Birds in Your Backyard.* New York: Avenel Book Co., 1949.

Pogtge, F. L. "Sassafras." *Pennsylvania Game News.* 46, no. 7 (1975). 17-19.

Robins, C. S., B. Bruun, and H. S. Zim. *A Guide of Field Identification of Birds of North America.* New

York: Golden Press, 1983.

Root, Terry. "An Analysis of Christmas Bird Count Data." *Atlas of Wintering North American Birds.* Chicago: University of Chicago Press, 1988.

Rose, Graham. *The Classic Garden*. New York: Summit Books, 1989.

Schultz, W. E. *How to Attract, House, and Feed Birds.* New York: Macmillan Co., 1970.

Seebohm, Caroline, and Christoper Simon Sykes. *Private Landscapes.* New York: Clarkson N. Potter, Inc., 1989.

Simpson, Benny J. *A Field Guide to Texas Trees.* Houston, Texas: Gulf Publishing, 1989.

Staff of the Liberty Hyde Bailey Hortorium. Initially compiled by Liberty Hyde Bailey and Ethel Zone Bailey. *Hortus Third.* New York: Macmillan Publishing Co., 1976.

Stiles, Edmund W. "Fruit for All Seasons." *Natural History.* 93, no. 8 (August 1984). 42-52.

Stokes, Donald W., and Lillian Q. Stokes. "In the Wild and at Your Feeder." *A Guide to Bird Behavior Volume 2*. Boston: Little, Brown and Company, 1983.

Stokes, Donald W., and Lillian Q. Stokes. *The Hummingbird Book*. Boston: Little, Brown and Company, 1989.

Vines, Robert A. *Trees, Shrubs, and Woody Vines of the Southwest.* Austin, Texas: University of Texas Press, 1960.

Wasowski, Sally, and Julie Ryan. *Landscaping with Native Texas Plants.* Austin, Texas: Texas Monthly Press, 1985.

Welch, William C. *Perennial Garden Color*. Dallas, Texas: Taylor Publishing Company, 1989.

Wetmore, Alexander. *Song and Garden Birds of North America.* Washington, D.C.: National Geographic Society, 1964.

# Index

# Index

HQ ADULT
761781
598.2973 POPE
Pope, T. E. (Thomas Everett),
1930-
Attracting birds to southern
gardens /